Ratios Made Simple

A beginner's guide to the key financial ratios

Robert Leach FCCA ACA

HARRIMAN HOUSE LTD

3A Penns Road
Petersfield
Hampshire
GU32 2EW
GREAT BRITAIN

Tel: +44 (0)1730 233870
Fax: +44 (0)1730 233880
Email: enquiries@harriman-house.com
Website: www.harriman-house.com

First published in Great Britain in 2010
Copyright © Harriman House Ltd

The right of Robert Leach to be identified as Author has been asserted
in accordance with the Copyright, Design and Patents Act 1988.

ISBN: 978-1906659-84-4

British Library Cataloguing in Publication Data
A CIP catalogue record for this book can be obtained from the British Library.

Designated trademarks and brands are the property of their respective owners.

Printed and bound by the CPI Group, Antony Rowe

Contents

About the Author   v

Introduction   vii

1. Profitability Ratios   1
   1.1. Earnings Per Share (EPS)   3
   1.2. Price-to-Earnings Ratio (P/E)   13
   1.3. Enterprise Value/Earnings Before Interest, Taxes,
       Depreciation and Amortisation Ratio (EV/EBITDA)   21
   1.4. Price-to-Sales Ratio (PSR)   25

2. Investment Ratios   29
   2.1. Dividend Yield   31
   2.2. Total Return   37
   2.3. Return On Capital Employed (ROCE)   41
   2.4. Return On Equity (ROE)   47
   2.5. Premium to Asset Value (PAV)   51
   2.6. Internal Rate of Return (IRR)   55
   2.7. Return On Assets (ROA)   59
   2.8. Dividend Payout Ratio   61

3. Dividend Cover   63
   3.1. Dividend Cover   65

4. Margins   69
   4.1. Gross Margin and Net Margin   71
   4.2. Overheads to Turnover   77

5. Gearing   79
   5.1. Gearing Ratio   81
   5.2. Interest Cover   89

6. Solvency Ratios   93
   6.1. Acid Test   95
   6.2. Current Ratio   99
   6.3. Cash Burn   101
   6.4. Defensive Interval   105
   6.5. Fixed Charges Cover   107

7. Efficiency Ratios   109
   7.1. Stock Turn   111
   7.2. Price-to-Book Value (PBV)   115
   7.3. Overtrading and Undertrading   117
   7.4. Item Comparison   121

8. Policy Ratios   125
   8.1. Creditor Period   127
   8.2. Debtor Period   131
   8.3. Fixed Asset Spending Ratio   133

9. Volatility   137
   9.1. Volatility Ratio   139
   9.2. Standard Deviation   143

Appendix   149
Index   155

About the Author

Robert Leach FCCA ACA is a chartered accountant, lecturer and author of more than 40 books, mainly on financial topics. His books include *The Investor's Guide to Understanding Accounts*. For two years he was a judge of the Stock Exchange Awards for best published accounts. He has written encyclopaedias on tax and payroll, and also writes for newsletters, magazines, newspapers and anyone else who will pay him.

Introduction

What is a ratio?

A ratio is simply one number divided by another. In financial terms, an accounting ratio is (usually) one figure from a set of accounts divided by another figure.

As even the simplest balance sheet and profit and loss (P&L) account is likely to contain at least 50 figures, there is a potential to produce 2500 ratios just from these two financial statements. This is before we look at other statements and the notes to the accounts. However, many of these ratios would be meaningless. Only a few ratios produce a number which will assist an investor.

This book lists the main ratios in categories of what they are indicating. These categories are listed in approximate order of relevance to the investor. Each ratio is defined and explained, before comment is given on how an investor should use it. Where alternatives to the ratios (or variations on them) exist these are indicated throughout the text.

Calculating ratios from company accounts

When calculating any ratio, make sure that you use the group accounts or consolidated accounts of the company. (These have the same meaning.) Almost all companies now operate as a group of companies. That means there is a holding company which itself owns shares in other companies known as subsidiaries. Often these subsidiaries have their own subsidiaries, known as sub-subsidiaries. This creates a family tree which can often have more than 100 companies in it. This is known as a group of companies. By law, the holding company must publish a separate set of accounts, but these are of no interest to the investor and should be ignored.

Copies of the accounts of a listed public company are usually put on the company's website, which can easily be found by typing the company's name into Google or any other search engine. The website may have a section for investors which includes all annual accounts for several years, with half-yearly reports and other announcements. Published accounts may also be requested from the company directly. Many companies also offer their accounts through the free Annual Reports Service, based in Surbiton: www.orderannualreports.com Ratios may generally be applied to smaller private companies. The accounts of smaller firms are not so readily available as those of larger firms, except that they must be filed at Companies House from where they are available to the public for a fee. In practice, if you are invited to invest in a private company, the existing shareholders will provide you with the accounts and much extra information also.

When ratios are calculated, figures are taken from the balance sheet or P&L account. In addition, many ratios require you to know other figures such as the share price, which can be found from the *Financial Times* or from many other publications and websites.

The accounts include other financial statements, such as cash flow statements, in addition to narrative reports and notes to the accounts. These are all important to the investor, but are little use in calculating ratios.

Understanding a ratio

A ratio by itself is usually a meaningless number. Knowing that the working capital ratio of a company is 1.3 tells you nothing about whether the company is a good investment or not. It does not even tell you whether a company is financially sound. Such a ratio means different things in different sectors.

A ratio must almost always be compared with other companies, or a trend must be reviewed, for it to be useful. A *comparison* is usually made with similar-sized companies in the same general industry. A *trend* is observed by looking at the same ratio for the same company in different years; an investor may sometimes plot the same ratio for the same company in different years to detect a trend.

Observing trends in this way is fine for established companies, but can be a problem for young companies. It is generally impossible to establish any trend for the first three years of a company's existence. Even after that, a young company's ratios can be volatile, as small changes in performance can lead to large changes in ratio figures.

Each ratio is intended to assist the process of identifying some aspect of a company, such as its profitability, efficiency or liquidity. Calculating all the possible ratios for all companies is likely to be tedious. Even if all the ratios are calculated for a company, many will not reveal anything of significance.

In calculating a ratio, you must remember that almost all accounts have an element of opinion. Someone will have had to provide estimated answers to questions such as:

- What is the value of this property?
- How many years will this machinery last?
- Will this debtor pay their bill?

All of these opinions are reflected in the accounts you use. If the directors' (or their accountants') opinions are wrong, your accounting ratios will similarly be wrong.

As mentioned above, accounting ratios rely heavily on the principle of comparability of different companies and of single companies through time. Changes in accounting standards, such as the widespread adoption of fair value accounting, can have the effect of distorting comparability.

If you are looking at a ratio, ensure you make use of what it tells you. Ratios can be effective as early indicators of problems. The company will always be able to spin a story as to why this is not a problem. Remember that the spin doctor has a motive; your calculator does not.

How investors should use ratios

In all cases, before investing in a company the investor must know what that company does. Never invest in anything you do not understand. If you do not know what a hedge fund or reinsurance company does, do not even consider investing in one until you find out. Understanding the company's activity is an essential prerequisite to understanding accounting ratios and to other aspects of investment policy-making.

> **There is no ratio that tells you whether a company is a good investment.**

It is not possible to perform a calculation which tells you how good the company is as an investment. Ratios may indicate that a company is profitable, growing, pays good dividends, is saving enough, is well-managed and so on. This can all be useful information, but none of these factors indicate that the company is a good investment.

Be wary about thinking that accounting ratios will help you discover some investment opportunity that everyone else has overlooked. The large companies have their accounts and other data (not all of which is readily accessible to the private investor) scrutinised by experienced analysts using sophisticated computer systems. It is unlikely that you will discover anything that they have not. For small companies, there is much more scope for such a discovery, but that must be offset against the fact that small companies are usually under the control of a few directors and shareholders who can dictate a change of policy easily.

There is also a danger of over-analysing accounts. An investor can become a *ratio junkie* who spends more time analysing company accounts than investing in companies. Many successful investors ignore ratios completely, or only use a few. Conversely, many analysts make poor investments. Understand the limitations of ratios. They are never more than just one tool in the investor's toolbox.

For the sake of completeness, most investment ratios likely to be encountered are included in this book. This does not mean that they are all recommended for use by private investors. Also bear in mind that many ratios are capable of different interpretations. So it is usually necessary for more than one ratio to be considered at a time.

A final point to remember is that a good company does not always mean a good investment.

> **A good investment is a company which you think will perform better than the market does.**

A good investment may actually be a poorly performing company. If the market thinks a company will perform worse than you think it will, that is a good investment.

Every investor must determine their investment strategy. This is likely to include:

- In what sectors will I invest?

- Am I looking primarily for dividend income or capital growth?

- How much time will I spend monitoring my investments?

- How much risk am I prepared to take? How far can I diversify away my risk?

- Am I looking for long-term growth or shorter-term gains?

There are no correct answers to any of these questions. Each investor must prepare their own investment strategy based on their own circumstances, abilities and finances.

Accounting ratios will assist you in meeting your investment strategy, but they are only ever part of the answer.

1

Profitability Ratios

1.1
Earnings Per Share (EPS)

Basic information and calculating the ratio

Definition

```
Earnings per share (EPS) = Net profit ÷ number of issued
                                                    shares
```

Net profit is the company's profit after payments of interest, tax and minority interests, but before payment of dividends to ordinary shareholders. In other words, the figure used for net profit is what is available to the holders of the company's ordinary shares from that year's profits.

If the company has made a loss during the accounting period, EPS is shown as a negative figure.

Interest includes all forms of payment on loans, preference shares and all other forms of borrowing or debt equity.

Tax means corporation tax that is or will be payable by the company on its profits for that period. Under tax law, some of that tax may not be payable until a future year. For accounting purposes, tax is calculated regardless of when it is payable, as that money is not otherwise available to the company and so needs to be set aside.

Minority interests means that part of the company's subsidiaries which it does not own. Suppose you own shares in *Company A* which owns 90% of the shares of *Company B*. This means that *Company B* is a subsidiary of *Company A*. However, 10% of *Company B* is not owned by your company. This 10% is reflected in the accounts as minority interest.

Number of shares means the weighted average of issued ordinary shares for the accounting period. The number of shares which a company is authorised to issue is not relevant.

Suppose a company had 1 million issued shares for the first two months of the accounting period, and 1.1 million shares for the remaining ten months. The weighted average is:

```
1 million x 2 months = 2 million

1.1 million x 10 months = 11 million

2 million + 11 million = 13 million
```

Therefore:

```
Weighted average = 13 million ÷ 12 months = 1.083 million
```

This figure is used even though there was no point in the year when the company had 1.083 million issued shares. The first two months' profits were earned by holders of 1 million shares, whereas the last ten months' profits were earned by holders of 1.1 million shares. Provided the profits were earned fairly evenly throughout the accounting period, the weighted average gives a fair approximation of the amount earned by each share.

Additional complications of the number of shares figure

The example given above is when additional shares were issued by the company during the year, such as in an equity issue, rights issue or conversion of another financial instrument. It is possible for the number of shares to reduce during the year, such as where a company buys back its shares. The weighted average of the number of shares is still used in these circumstances.

Where the value of shares changes in a bonus issue, share split or share consolidation, the weighted average is not used. Suppose a company has 2 million shares, each of which has a value of £48. The company may decide to split the shares so that there are 20 million shares with a value of £4.80 each. A weighted average here would give a meaningless figure and so the EPS is calculated on the basis that there were 20 million shares throughout the whole period.

This principle is followed even when the bonus issue, share split or share consolidation happened *after* the date of the balance sheet. EPS is calculated on the *number* of shares at the balance sheet date, but the *size* of the share when the accounts are subsequently published.

Diluted EPS

Diluted EPS is a second figure which is sometimes given. This recalculates the EPS on the basis that anything which may become an ordinary share has done so.

Suppose a company has 10 million issued ordinary shares. It has also issued share options and convertible preference shares. If all the options were exercised and all the preference shares converted, the company would have 12 million issued ordinary shares. This will reduce the value of earnings per share.

When is diluted EPS stated?

Under accounting standard FRS 14 (explained below), diluted EPS only needs to be stated if it differs from the normal EPS by 5% or more. (This 5% rule does not apply to IAS 33, so accounts produced under International Accounting Standards must always show diluted EPS, however small the difference.)

EPS is a factual figure; diluted EPS is a hypothetical figure.

Calculation of EPS can be performed from figures in the published balance sheet. However, the investor does not have to do this calculation. The EPS is the one accounting ratio which the company itself is required to calculate and publish in its accounts.

The duty to publish derives from Financial Reporting Standard **FRS 14**, which has legal force under company law. FRS 14 only applies to shares which are (or are due to be) publicly traded.

FRS 14 applies for all accounting periods which ended after 22 December 1998. Prior to this, EPS was calculated according to Statement of Standard Accounting Practice SSAP 3, introduced in 1972. This standard was amended in 1974 to reflect a change in the tax system, and in 1993 (by FRS 3) which in effect abolished extraordinary items in accounts. In 1997, International Accounting Standard IAS 33 was published on the subject of EPS. After consultation, the Accounting Standards Board decided broadly to implement this standard in the UK as FRS 14.

It should be noted that EPS is not readily comparable between companies because accounting practice allows considerable latitude to company directors and accountants on what they include in net profit.

Internationally, the issue of IAS 33 and UK adoption of FRS 14 has brought some harmonisation between UK and other national accounting standards on EPS. It has also narrowed the differences between UK and US calculations. However, there are still some differences between countries on how EPS is calculated.

FRS 14 and IAS 33, like all accounting standards, only state the *minimum* disclosure that a company must make. A company may make further disclosures and should do so if this would help users of the accounts. There may be other items in the profit and loss account which a company wishes to state as so *much per share*. A company may do this, but must make it clear that this is not the statutory EPS figure, and must produce a reconciliation of how this other figure equates to the statutory EPS.

Understanding EPS

EPS indicates the profitability of the company from the shareholders' perspective. It is a figure widely used in financial analysis. EPS is also part of the widely used price-to-earnings (P/E) ratio, as explained below.

Unlike almost all other accounting ratios, EPS is an amount of money and not just a number. If a company has net profit of £20 million and has 2 million issued shares, the EPS is £10.

The net profit wholly belongs to the ordinary shareholders of the company. It is calculated on the basis that everyone else has been paid: all taxes, interest on bank loans, dividends on preference shares, creditors and so on. What is left of the net profit is there to reward the ordinary shareholders for their investment.

It is possible for the company to pay the whole of this amount to the shareholders. In our example, each share would pay a dividend of £10. In practice, this is unlikely. The company will almost always want some **retained profit** to fund its future activities, such as buying more machinery and more stock, and paying for more marketing.

It may also want to put aside some money into **reserves**. These are funds where cash is squirrelled away for a specific purpose, such as to acquire new businesses, to develop new products or to replace existing plant. It may also want some money to buy back its own shares. Any sensible business also wishes to keep some money as general security, as a buffer against the uncertainties of commercial activity.

How a company decides to share out its net profit between dividends, retained profit, or reserves is a matter of commercial judgment for the directors. Whether that share-out is wise is a matter of investor judgment for you.

But EPS ignores all these considerations. Whatever a company decides to do with the net profit should be for the financial benefit of the ordinary shareholders. The dividends provide an immediate cash benefit; retained profit is used to help the company make future profits from which future dividends are paid and which maintain the value of the share. EPS makes no distinction between these two forms of benefit to the shareholder.

EPS looks to the past, not to the future

The backward-looking nature of EPS was considered by the Accounting Standards Board when writing FRS 14. For example, the calculations for diluted EPS use the average ordinary share price for the accounting period rather than the period-end market price. The ASB did consider introducing an element of the future into EPS (mainly in relation to diluted EPS) but concluded that it was not possible to satisfy the dual function of a forward-looking objective with historic data.

How to use EPS as an investor

EPS has three main uses for the investor. It is used to:

1. indicate return on investment

2. indicate a company's retained profit, and

3. calculate the profit-to-earnings (P/E) ratio.

By itself, EPS is a fairly meaningless figure. Knowing that an ordinary share has an EPS of £1.37 for an accounting period tells you nothing about how well the company is doing. Nor does it tell you whether it is a good investment. As with most ratios, EPS only has meaning when compared to another figure, such as the share's value, how much you paid for it or how much dividend you receive.

Suppose you spent £4 buying a share which has an EPS of 60p. This means that your £4 investment has earned you 60p, or 15%, that year. You may only receive perhaps 20p in cash as a dividend, but that means that the other 40p is being used by the business. Another way of looking at it is that you have earned 60p, of which 20p is paid to you immediately and the other 40p is reinvested in the business for you.

So the first use of EPS is to indicate **return on investment**. Chapter 1 explains that dividend yield looks at how much *dividend* you receive for your investment. In the example above, the dividend yield is 5%, namely 20p on a £4 purchase. EPS looks at the dividend in addition to the amount you have earned that has been reinvested on your behalf to keep the business going. In our example, this is 15% (60p out of £4).

In this example the EPS is 10% larger than the dividend yield. The additional 10% is in effect received by the shareholder in terms of the share's value. If the company has retained all those 40p amounts per shareholder, the company is worth more and has a greater ability to earn future dividends. If the company makes no profit in one year, part of that 40p could be used to pay a dividend.

This is not the traditional method of calculating return on investment, which considers only the amounts of actual cash that change hands. Seeing EPS as total return does introduce an element of future prospects, which is the main concern of any investor. It is always possible for the company to waste the other 40p of non-dividend earnings. That is a matter of judgment for the investor to form about the company. The EPS alerts you to the need to make such a judgment.

The second use of EPS is to indicate **retained profit**. This can be done by comparing dividend with EPS. In our example, the company distributed just one-third of its available profit and retained the other two-thirds. This indicates a commitment to long-term growth, in the absence of any indicators to the contrary.

An investor usually looks for either long-term growth or short-term gain, or an appropriate mixture. In general, the lower the dividend is relative to EPS, the more likely it is that the share represents long-term growth.

This is a sweeping generalisation of what really requires a much deeper analysis. A company in severe difficulties may pay a small dividend relative to its EPS because it desperately needs the cash to get itself out of trouble. This is exactly the situation of several banks in 2009. However, this generalisation is convenient as it involves a simple calculation of two readily available figures. In many cases, it will give the right answer, and in other cases it will indicate when further analysis is required.

The third use of EPS is in **calculating the P/E ratio**, as explained in section 1.2.

Significance of a negative EPS

If a company makes a **loss**, its EPS is negative. This figure is only of significance for an established company. For a new start-up business which is still on *cash burn* of its original funding (see section 6.3), a negative EPS can be calculated, but the figure has no real meaning. There are other ratios which are more appropriate for start-ups.

Undiluted or diluted EPS

An investor needs to decide whether to use **diluted EPS** or the undiluted figure. Generally, use the undiluted figure unless the company is about to issue additional shares.

A significant difference between the two figures for EPS is itself significant. This is only likely to happen to smaller companies. An investor should ask why the company has issued so much convertible stock or so many share options. Convertible preference shares give the holders the best of both worlds – fixed returns when profits are uncertain, and the right to high returns if good profits are sustained. As these holders did not participate in the risk during periods of uncertain profits, their conversion rights are to the detriment of the ordinary shareholders who did participate in that risk. An ordinary shareholder should ask why a company needed to borrow so much money in terms which are disadvantageous to its owners.

Smoothing out of EPS by a company

An investor should be aware that a company has some scope for smoothing out the EPS. Methods include:

- changing the amounts in provisions

- changing the policy on writing down old stock

- including intangible assets on the balance sheet

- revaluation of assets

- changing the depreciation policy, and

- repatriating foreign profits.

Variation of EPS over time

An investor should always be wary of accounts where the EPS shows less variation than other investment and profit ratios. Points to look out for are:

- Changes in accounting policy which are not explained or where the explanation lacks credibility.

- Any indication (from the accounts or from other sources) that the company could face an unwelcome takeover – all financial reports become suspect in a hostile takeover.

- Reporting a profit slightly above the previous year. This may indicate that the profits have been massaged by using reserves and similar methods. In such a case, the profits are likely to plunge in the following year.

1.2
Price-to-Earnings Ratio (P/E)

Basic information and calculating the ratio

Definition

```
Price/Earnings = Share price ÷ earnings per share
```

Share price is the mid-market price of the share at the close of business on the previous trading day. This can usually be read from the *Financial Times* or a similar publication.

Earnings per share (EPS) is calculated as explained earlier in this chapter.

Understanding P/E Ratio

The P/E ratio is, by far, the commonest ratio for investors. It is so common that it is routinely listed in daily lists of share prices. In practice, a P/E ratio is only considered for a listed company making a profit.

This ratio is sometimes abbreviated as PER. It is also sometimes referred to as *earnings multiple* or even just *multiple*. Sometimes P/E is called *trailing P/E* to clarify that the EPS is of the last published 12-month period and not of another period. This can be abbreviated as P/E TTM (trailing 12 months). All of these different terms mean the same.

Only listed shares have a quoted share price, so the P/E is rarely used for **unlisted companies** or those whose shares are not readily traded. If a P/E is attempted for such a company, some mechanism must be established for determining a realistic price.

A company that makes a **loss** has a negative EPS. Mathematically this would produce a negative P/E, but such a figure is never quoted as it has no real meaning. If a company makes a loss, it is regarded as not having a P/E and other ratios or measures must be considered instead.

The P/E ratio is sometimes seen as representing the number of years' profits it will take for the share price to be earned. If a share value is £6 and the EPS is 60p, the P/E is 10. In ten years, the shareholder will have earned the value of the share. There are many faults with this approach (such as the fact that the shareholder still owns the share after ten years).

It is probably better to see the P/E ratio as a simple yardstick reflecting market confidence in the share. Mathematically it strips out factors relating to the size because a huge company and a tiny company can easily have the same P/E.

The higher the P/E is, the more confidence the market has in that company. It is as simple as that. Share prices are determined by supply and demand. So popularity of a share pushes up the share value and thus pushes up the P/E.

The share price is a factor of how the market thinks the company *will* perform whereas EPS is a factor of how the company *has* performed. A high P/E indicates that the market believes the company will improve.

Until the 1980s, a P/E rarely rose much above 20. Indeed for the twentieth century, the average P/E ratio was 16 (or 14 if you use a geometric mean rather than the arithmetic mean). Since the 1980s, there has been a growing incidence of much higher P/E ratios. The *Financial Times* does not publish any P/E above 80 as it believes that such large numbers are meaningless.

How to use P/E as an investor

Unlike most other ratios, the P/E ratio may be considered in **isolation** – to a point.

It is not possible to be too specific about what a P/E means in isolation, but the very general guide in Table 1 may be regarded as a good starting point.

Table 1 – General guide to interpreting P/E values

P/E range	Implications of P/E
Below 10	The market has some concern about the company. It may believe the company is in terminal decline or there is some other reason why the market does not like the company.
10-18	This indicates that the company is probably fairly valued.
18-30	The market expects the company to do extremely well, or the shares are overvalued.
Above 30	This is suspicious. It indicates that the market has an exceptionally high opinion of future share growth. Such a company could be a bubble that explodes, as happened with many dotcom companies in 1999. An investor should always look to see why the market has such a high view of that company and how realistic this is.

A P/E does not in itself say whether a company is a good investment. The P/E tells you very simply what the market thinks. A good investment is one which you reasonably believe will perform better than the market thinks it will. After a while, you can get a feel for what you believe the P/E of a company should be.

> A good investment is where you believe the P/E is too low.

A high P/E does not mean a good investment (a common fallacy). The low P/E indicates a possible potential for a good investment, but no more.

Many investment analysts look at companies with average P/E rather than high P/E or low P/E. An average P/E can indicate that the company is performing well but still has capacity for growth.

Smaller stocks tend to have a higher P/E. The current average P/E for a FTSE 100 company is 13, whereas for a FTSE 250 company (the 101st to 350th largest companies listed on the London Stock Exchange), the average P/E is 19 – about 1½ times as much. This reflects the fact that these mid-cap companies tend to attract private equity interest.

Interpreting the P/E of companies in different sectors

Another application is as a quick **comparison** with other shares, even in different industries. The P/E ratio makes building shares, pharmaceutical shares and leisure sector shares directly comparable as a single number.

Unlike many other ratios, the **industrial sector** has little influence on P/E, though it still has some influence. Unpopular sectors, such as tobacco, tend to have a lower P/E because their unpopularity depresses their share value. Pharmaceutical shares tend to have a higher P/E because their research and development expenditure is written off and not capitalised, which depresses their EPS.

The oil industry is an interesting example: the P/E is often a low figure around 12. As oil is expected to have a demand outstripping supply, pushing up prices and thus earnings, it would be reasonable to expect oil companies to have a high P/E. The truth is that the market regards the high levels of oil price as being unsustainable (and volatile).

Comparing investments in shares with other investments using P/E

A final application is as a comparison with **other investments**. If you divide 100 by the P/E, the answer gives you a number which is comparable as a percentage total return on the current value of your shareholding.

For example, you bought a share for £4 that is now worth £5. It has an EPS of 25p. This gives it a P/E of 20 (£5 ÷ 25p). Note that the price you paid for the share is not considered. You could sell your share or buy more shares that day for £5 and so that is the relevant value for comparison. If you divide 100 by 20, you get 5%. So the P/E indicates that the investment is roughly comparable to an investment providing a 5% annual return.

This is not entirely accurate, as it ignores the continuing value of the share itself, among other things. However, it does provide a very quick rule-of-thumb for comparing investments. If making a decision involving a significant sum, it is necessary to take a more detailed analytical approach. Nevertheless, there is still a direct correlation. When gilt returns are high, P/E ratios tend to fall.

Variations on P/E ratio

There are many variations on the P/E ratio which are briefly noted here.

PEG is the price/earnings to growth ratio. It is calculated by dividing the P/E by the annual growth rate.

The significance of PEG is that the annual growth rate is the main reason for a higher P/E ratio. The PEG strips out this factor to produce a lower number which indicates what the market thinks of the share other than its growth potential. The PEG gives a lower figure than P/E.

Forward P/E is the P/E but using the estimated EPS for the next accounting period. As this involves an element of guesswork, the forward P/E is not always reliable. This is sometimes abbreviated as P/Ef or called *estimated P/E*.

P/E from continued operations reduces EPS by stripping out those elements of earnings from anything other than a continuing operation. So it removes profits from discontinued activities, windfalls, extraordinary items, write-downs and non-trading profits. This gives a number bigger than the P/E ratio. This ratio is only of value if the company has significant repeated income from sources other than continuing operations.

P/E 10 replaces EPS for the last year with the average EPS for the past ten years. The longer the period considered, the more stable share price changes tend to be. There is evidence that shares tend to remain constant over a 20-year period, so the last ten years indicates the next ten. This assumes that the company is still being run in the same manner.

E/P divides EPS by share value. It is simply the P/E ratio the other way round. The answer is the reciprocal of the P/E, so if the P/E is 10, the E/P is 0.1. This allows comparison with other forms of investment, particularly gilts. The principle is the same as dividing 100 by the P/E, as explained above.

Market P/E calculates the P/E ratio not for a share but for an entire market, sector or share index. This involves converting each company's EPS to a factor relevant to its original EPS and weighting this according to the company's size. This is exactly the same process used in calculating share indices such as the FTSE 100 index. The *market P/E* is the average P/E for all companies in that market, sector or index. This allows a direct comparison with the P/E of each individual company.

During the twentieth century market P/E has approximately doubled from 10 to 20 with most of the increase in the last 20 years. This has continued into the twenty-first century. This probably reflects the greater realisation of potential for share investment.

There is a view that when the market P/E rises above 18, the market needs a correction (that is, a fall). This happened in 1997, early 1998 and in 2006, each of which was followed by a fall.

Present Value of Growth Opportunities (PVGO) is not a variation on P/E as it uses a completely different methodology, but it attempts to measure the same thing. PVGO rises in a manner similar to P/E.

The formula is:

```
PVGO = [D/(r-g)] - E/r
```

Where:

```
D = the dividend for the next period

r = the cost of capital or the capitalisation rate of the
                                                    company

E = earning on equity (EPS)

g = the growth rate of the company
```

This is a complicated formula where some of the elements are not readily quantifiable. For this reason, PVGO is not normally a ratio fit for use by investors.

1.3
Enterprise Value/Earnings Before Interest, Taxes, Depreciation and Amortisation Ratio (EV/EBITDA)

Basic information and calculating the ratio

Definition

```
EV/EBITDA ratio = enterprise value ÷ EBITDA
```

Enterprise value is the current value of a business, taking into account its debt. It is calculated using this formula:

```
Enterprise value = market capitalisation + total debt -
                                            total cash
```

Market capitalisation is the current value of the business as recognised by a stock market. This is represented by the formula:

```
Market capitalisation = number of equity shares x share
                                                   price
```

The EV/EBITDA figure is often given in lists of quoted companies.

The enterprise value is a measure of what the company is worth. The adjustment for debt and cash reflects the fact that the company is partly funded by its borrowings. It allows companies to be valued on a comparable basis when they are funded differently.

Debt is added back on the EV side and interest on debt is added back on the EBITDA side.

EBITDA stands for earnings before interest, tax, depreciation and amortisation. **Depreciation** is the amount by which the value of fixed assets (such as buildings, vehicles, plant and furniture) is reduced during the year. **Amortisation** is the amount by which purchased goodwill is reduced. This is the amount of a business bought by a company which exceeds the value of its net assets.

Company reports may refer to EBITDA. Otherwise, the easiest way to establish the EBITDA is to look for net profit before interest and tax, and add back the figure or figures for depreciation and amortisation.

Understanding EV/EBITDA

EV/EBITDA is a measure that is used for companies which are no longer start-ups but are not yet earning enough profit to be self-sustaining. It is a modified form of P/E ratio for companies which do not have any profits.

For such companies, it is also appropriate to consider the price-to-sales ratio (discussed below) and cash burn (discussed in Chapter 6).

EBITDA is a measure used by companies making a gross profit but not a net profit. Any mention of EBITDA indicates that the company is not yet profitable, but sees a positive EBITDA as a milestone on the way.

As a figure, EBITDA ranks between gross profit and net profit. It still deducts the expenses which relate to being in business, such as rates, power, insurance and office staff. It excludes the finance charges of interest, tax, depreciation and amortisation. The last two of these do not even involve any cash changing hands.

EBITDA is often overrated, particularly by directors who promote a positive EBITDA to conceal a net loss. A positive EBITDA is like a person saying that they are living within their means, if they exclude their mortgage, loan repayments and income tax. The truth is that they are not living within their means and neither is a company with a positive EBITDA that is making a net loss.

How to use EV/EBITDA as an investor

The extent to which EV/EBITDA provides any useful information at all to an investor is debatable. Despite this, the ratio is now widely used.

This ratio is only used for companies not making a profit and in these circumstances Price-to-Sales ratio (below) and cash burn (Chapter 6) will usually give more relevant information.

The investor must never believe that EBITDA is the equivalent of net profit and should always be sceptical of any report which relies on EBITDA.

In so far as the investor believes that this ratio provides any useful information, it should be interpreted in a similar manner to P/E ratio, in that a higher number indicates greater market optimism for the company.

1.4
Price-to-Sales Ratio (PSR)

Definition

```
Price-to-Sales ratio = Market capitalisation ÷ annual
                                                   sales
```

Price-to-sales ratio is sometimes abbreviated to PSR or called the **revenue multiple**.

The ratio can also be calculated by dividing the share price by the sales per share.

Market capitalisation is the current value of the business as recognised by a stock market. This is represented by the formula:

```
Market capitalisation = number of equity shares x share
                                                    price
```

This figure is often given in lists of quoted companies.

The **share price** is the figure listed in the *Financial Times* or similar publication. The definition is the same as for the P/E ratio.

Annual sales is the **turnover** of the business. It is sometimes called the **revenue** or just **sales**.

Understanding PSR

PSR is a simple measure of how many years of a company's sales the market value of the company represents. Ultimately, every asset is simply a source of producing wealth. A lathe costing £20,000 is cost-justified in that it will generate at least £20,000 of additional profit. If it did not, the company should not buy the lathe.

More on market capitalisation and the value of a company

The market capitalisation represents how much the stock market thinks a company is worth.

In turn, this may be represented by the formula:

```
Market capitalisation = net assets + goodwill
```

If a company says it is worth £100 million you should be able to look at the accounts to ask *"Where is this £100 million?"* The balance sheet will tell you how much the company owns in terms of land, buildings, plant, vehicles, furniture, investments, cash, debtors and other forms of asset. From this, you subtract the net liabilities, namely creditors. This gives the figure for **net assets.**

Goodwill is the term for the rest of the value of a business. A trading company is worth more than its net assets. It has the benefit of experienced staff, its reputation and all the marketing to date, in addition to having established relationships and procedures. This additional value is known as the goodwill of a business. The term comes from the days when a trader sold his business and made known his goodwill to the new owner.

In valuing a business for sale, it is common to value goodwill as a multiple of net profits. The multiple corresponds to the return desired by the investor. It is possible to produce an accounting ratio of goodwill divided by net profit, but no one does as what it would tell you is better expressed by other ratios.

How to use PSR as an investor

The PSR can indicate how cheap a company's shares are. Unlike P/E and EPS, it can be calculated for almost any company, even those making a loss.

The PSR ratio is sometimes used as an alternative to the P/E ratio, where the company is either making a loss or the P/E ratio does not give a meaningful answer for another reason. PSR is widely used for start-up companies.

As a rule of thumb, a PSR of below 1 indicates that the shares are cheap, particularly when they are significantly below 1. Research by economists suggests that an extended PSR of below 1 is a reliable indicator that a company's shares will increase in value.

This is tempered by the fact that the ratio is dividing an opinion (what the market thinks the shares are worth) by fact (the annual sales). This is also true of P/E and EPS. This means that the PSR depends on market opinion. If the market opinion is that a share will increase in value, that has an immediate effect on the current value. In this sense, the PSR, like all these profitability ratios, becomes a self-fulfilling prophecy. Market opinion reflects future prospects.

2

Investment Ratios

2.1
Dividend Yield

Definition:

```
Dividend yield = dividend ÷ share price
```

This figure is usually expressed as a percentage, which means multiplying the above by 100. The dividend yield is often simply called **yield**.

Dividend is the total of dividends paid for the year, grossed up to allow for the rate of tax deducted at source. The dividend is often paid twice a year. There is an interim dividend paid during the trading year, followed by a final dividend paid about six months later. Some companies pay dividends four times a year. There is no law about how many times dividends should be paid.

The figure for dividends is those for the last period of 12 months. Where dividends are paid twice a year, the dividend side of the formula changes twice a year. This is when the shares go *ex div* instead of *cum div*. This is indicated in share listings as **xd** or **cd**.

The amount of a dividend is announced a short while before it is paid. This allows the registrar to calculate the amount of dividend payable to each shareholder and to arrange the payments. Suppose a dividend is payable on 1 March. The share may go ex div on 14 February. This means that if a share in that company is sold between those dates, the dividend is paid to the seller and not to the buyer. There is usually a small drop in value of a share when a dividend is announced.

Grossed up means multiplied by a factor to represent the tax deducted at source. UK dividends are currently subject to 10% income tax deducted at source. This means that the figure must be grossed up by 11.11%. Note that this is a different rate from the basic rate of 20% that otherwise applies.

Suppose you receive £100 in dividends. Since 1999, this is grossed up by 11.11% (one-ninth) to £111.11. Tax at 10% on this figure is £11.11, which brings you back to £100. Note that this 11.11% rate is used even when the shareholder is not liable to pay tax or when the shareholder is liable to pay higher rate tax.

Share price is as stated in the *Financial Times* or similar list of shares. These published lists of shares will often also give the dividend yield.

Understanding dividend yield

Dividend yield is simply how much your shares are earning you as an investment. The dividend yield is the amount of regular income as measured by the current *worth* of your investment in that company.

A **dividend** is that part of the profits that the directors decide to pass to the shareholders. It is sometimes also called a distribution. Suppose a company makes £10 million profit and has 20 million shareholders. The directors decide to keep £7 million as retained profit for their further use, and distribute £3 million as dividend. That means that each share earns a dividend of 15p. If you own 1000 shares, you will receive a cheque for £150.

As the dividend is paid from profits after the company has paid **tax**, the amount received by the shareholder is regarded as tax paid. This means that a basic rate taxpayer does not have to pay any more tax on the dividend. Someone who does not pay tax (because they are on a low income, for example) cannot reclaim any tax on the dividend.

A higher rate taxpayer, who pays income tax up to 40%, is liable to pay income tax at a rate of 32.5% on the grossed up figure. If a higher rate taxpayer receives a dividend of £100 he is liable to pay tax at 32.5% on the grossed up figure of £111.11, of which £11.11 has already been paid. So the tax liability is £36.11, from which £11.11 is deducted, so an additional £25 is payable by the shareholder.

Tax on shares may be reclaimed if the shares are held in an individual savings account (ISA).

The dividend yield is sometimes simply called the **yield**. This figure is widely quoted. It is likely to be printed in the annual report. It also appears in the list of share values in *Financial Times* and similar lists. Dividend yield provides a measure of comparability between different types of investment.

To be precise, dividend yield reveals one of the two elements of how much your shares are earning you. Dividend yield looks at how much the dividends are earning you in terms of regular income. The other element of your earnings from the share is how much the share gains in value.

When dividend yield cannot be used

A share can only quote a dividend yield when the company is actually paying a dividend. Many companies go through periods of not paying a dividend at all. This applies during:

- the early years before the company has started to make a profit

- during a difficult period when the company decides to retain all its profits, and

- during a period when the company simply decides to go solely for capital growth.

When companies are not paying a dividend, other ratios and factors must be considered. Even for dividend-paying companies, yield is not always the whole story.

How to use dividend yield as an investor

The dividend yield is a simple single measure that allows different shares to be compared regardless of their size or sector. At its simplest, the higher the yield the better, though there are significant exceptions to this simple rule.

The dividend yield allows a simple comparison with **other investments**. A dividend that is paying 2% can be seen as producing a smaller income stream than another investment paying 5%. However, such a comparison must always allow for the fact that shares also earn a return in the form of capital growth. Typically shares pay less in dividend yield than other forms of investment.

It is also possible to use dividend yield to indicate the **health** of the company. Since 2000, UK shares have produced a typical dividend yield of around 3%. This may be regarded as the benchmark.

Shares with a higher yield may seem attractive, but this is often an indication that the market considers the dividend record to be unsustainable. Lloyds TSB had a dividend yield of 7% or more before it spectacularly crashed in 2009 and had to be bailed out by the government. If the dividend yield is above 3%, you should look to see how sustainable that record is, starting by considering dividend cover (as explained in Chapter 3).

A shareholder also needs to consider the **dividend record**. The fact that a company paid a good dividend in one year does not necessarily mean that it will pay such a dividend in the next year. It may earn good profits in one year and then much lower profits in the next year.

It should be remembered that the company quotes its dividend as so much per share. If it pays 10p per share in one year when the shares are worth £4 and pays 10p again next year when the shares are worth £5, the company is regarded as maintaining its dividend record, even though the yield has fallen from 2.5% to 2%.

In practice, companies often try to smooth out fluctuations in dividends by using profits from good years to make up for profits in bad years. Sometimes companies have a **dividend policy**. This may be stated in the annual report, or otherwise deduced from the dividend record. The two commonest dividend policies are to maintain dividends at a constant figure, or to increase the dividend slowly. For the latter, the increase is more likely to be added to the final dividend, leaving the interim dividend unchanged.

Variations on dividend yield

Future yield is calculated on the same basis as the dividend yield, but looks at the dividends expected to be paid in the next year, rather than those that have been paid in the past year.

2.2
Total Return

Definition

```
Total return = capital growth + dividend yield on
                                   purchase price
```

Capital growth is the increase in value of shares, measured as a percentage of the amount you paid for them. Suppose you originally bought £1000 worth of shares. At the start of a later year they are worth £1500 and at the end of that year they are worth £1600. The increase in value in that year is £100, which is 10% of the £1000 you paid. The capital growth is therefore 10%.

Dividend yield on purchase price is calculated as explained earlier in this chapter, except that you use your purchase price instead of the current price. In our example, suppose the dividend for the year was £30. That is 3% of the purchase price of £1000.

Mathematically, percentages may only be added if they are percentages of the same number. In our example, the percentages are 10% and 3%, so the total return is 13%.

Although this figure is calculated by adding rather than dividing, it may still be considered an accounting ratio as it adds two figures that are initially calculated by division.

Understanding total return

Total return equates the two elements by which investors obtain their return on shares: capital growth and dividends. These two elements are not always present. A share may have lost value but still be worth holding because of its high dividends. This is one reason why so many bank shares were still regarded as good investments before the economic crisis started in 2007. Other shares may pay no dividends but be held for their capital growth only.

Investment trusts are limited companies (despite their name) that invest in shares. As a collective investment, they are similar to unit trusts, except that you do own shares and an investment trust is usually less restricted. Investment trusts often split the income from their holdings into two companies, one for capital growth and one for dividend income.

How to use total return as an investor

Total return allows the investor to compare investments. In the example at the start of this section, the 13% return compares with the rather smaller investment usually obtained from a bank deposit account or building society.

Total return has the advantage of expressing in a single figure the reason you bought shares in the first place – to make a profit. As a measure of investment return, it is most appropriate when the investor is not particularly bothered whether the profit comes from growth or dividend.

It should be realised that these two elements have completely different investment profiles in addition to being taxed quite differently. Dividends are subject to income tax at source when paid, whereas capital growth is subject to capital gains tax but (usually) only when you sell the shares.

Variations on total return

Total return on current value

Total return on current value performs the same calculation as that for total return but substitutes in the figure for the start of the year for the purchase price. For example:

```
Total return on current value = capital growth + dividend
                          yield on price at year start
```

If the shares were bought some time ago, the total return can give a very high figure. This is because we have not allowed for inflation. This can be overcome be calculating both the capital growth and the dividend yield according to the share value one year ago.

Thinking back to our earlier example, the shares were worth £1500 each at the start of the year and £1600 at the end of the year. Therefore, the capital growth is £100 ÷ £1500, which is 6.7%.

We suggested that our share paid a dividend of £30, so the dividend yield is £30 on £1500, which is 2%. So the total return using current figures is 6.7% capital growth + 2% dividend yield, which is 8.7%.

This can be seen as providing a better comparator than total return on the basis that you could have sold the shares for £1500 at the start of the year, pocketing the capital growth to that point and could then have invested the money differently.

Overall return on current value

Overall return on current value performs the same calculation as total return on current value using the price, but then either divides the result by the number of years, or takes the root for the period. Division is simpler, but taking the root is more accurate.

The **root** of a number is the number which when multiplied enough times gives you the original answer. In this example, 1.118 multiplied five times gives 1.75 (allowing for rounding). This can be calculated by using the $x^{1/y}$ key on a mathematical calculator, or by entering =POWER(number,root) in an Excel spreadsheet and pressing the return key. In this example, you would type =POWER(1.75,0.2).

Suppose in our example the dividend has been £30 each year and the shares have been held for five years.

The capital growth for the period has been 1.6 (that is the shares have grown by 60% and are now worth 1.6 times as much). You have received a £30 dividend each year, or £150 for five years. This is a return of 0.15 on the price paid because you originally bought your shares for £1000. So the total return over the five-year period is capital growth of 1.6 + dividend yield of 0.15, which is 1.75. This means there has been an addition of 0.75 – the return is 75% over five years.

Then to find the overall return on current value you can divide this 75% return by 5, so that your average return for each of the five years is 0.15 or 15%.

To take the root, you must add 1, so we take the fifth root of 1.75. This is 1.118 (rounded to three decimal places), as calculated using a computer or calculator. To convert this to a decimal, we subtract 1 and multiply by 100.

```
(1.118 - 1) x 100 = 11.8%
```

This means that the share has earned us an average 11.8% over the five-year period. This figure is much more accurate than simple division. In this example, it shows a significantly lower figure than the approximation from division, which was 15%.

While taking a root gives an accurate answer, it is still open to the criticism that the dividend figures do not allow for inflation. £30 five years ago is worth more than £30 today. This could be allowed for by increasing past dividend figures by a factor representing inflation. However, before becoming such a maths anorak, you should ask yourself why you are trying to obtain such an accurate figure for total return.

2.3
Return On Capital Employed (ROCE)

Definition

```
ROCE = (profit before interest and tax ÷ net capital
                                   employed) x 100
```

ROCE is the standard abbreviation for return on capital employed. The number is usually multiplied by 100 to express it as a percentage.

Profit before interest and tax is taken from the profit and loss account. If the company has no borrowings and pays no interest, this is the pre-tax profit. Otherwise, you may have to subtract the interest figure from the pre-tax profit.

All interest must be excluded, including interest earned. If the interest earned is greater than the interest paid, the figure for profit before interest and tax is *greater* than the figure for pre-tax profit.

Net capital employed (NCE) is taken from the balance sheet. Sometimes the figure is simply stated on the balance sheet. Otherwise, it can be calculated in several ways. Probably the simplest method is to take the figure for all the assets on the balance sheet and to subtract the figure for current liabilities.

NCE is the total amount of capital the company has available. It comes from shareholders, profits, revaluations and long-term borrowings.

Understanding ROCE

ROCE is widely seen as an overall efficiency and profitability measure. It measures how well the directors are using the capital available to them.

The figure may be considered in isolation, or in comparison with the ROCE for comparable companies or for the same company in different periods. However, unlike many ratios, ROCE is not widely used to plot trends. If an investor is making an investment decision based on ROCE they are doing so because they want to know how profitable the company is now.

The main comparison for ROCE is against the cost of capital (as explained in Chapter 7). To ensure that a fair comparison is made, the figure for profit before interest and tax needs to be adjusted. This adjustment adds back the tax relief given on the interest paid. This adjusted figure is sometimes called NOPLAT for *net operating profit less adjusted taxes*.

ROCE can be significantly affected by intangible assets and written off goodwill. It may also be affected when a large part of the capital employed comprises short-term loans, such as bank overdrafts. If the figure for capital employed is the total as shown on the balance sheet, such financing is excluded as it is netted off against current assets on the balance sheet.

ROCE can also be significantly increased by any management policy that has the effect of reducing capital employed. Examples include:

- Not fully valuing property and other large assets.

- Writing off goodwill immediately on acquisition.

- Very generous depreciation policies.

- Not putting a separate value on intangibles such as brand names.

How to use ROCE as an investor

In general, a good company has a high ROCE and a bad company has a low ROCE. This means that ROCE is the nearest we get to a ratio which measures the merits of a company in a single figure.

A poorly performing company will have a small percentage figure for its ROCE. Such a company could easily fail in an economic downturn. If the ROCE is less than the cost of borrowing, any further borrowings will reduce the earnings per share. A company with a low ROCE is less likely to be taken over. A company performing well can easily have an ROCE of over 30%.

This generalisation needs some qualification. Where a business is cyclical, a company may indicate a low ROCE even though it is very profitable.

The investor should usually compare ROCE with cost of capital; ROCE should always be higher. If ROCE is lower than the cost of capital, the company is slowly destroying its capital base. Put more bluntly, the management is so inefficient that it is killing off the company.

Even if the ROCE is lower than the cost of capital, this does not necessarily make the company a bad investment (though, in reality, this is the usual conclusion). It is possible that an investor could conclude that the management will improve or change, or that the company's decay is not as bad as the market thinks.

This is in accordance with the fundamental investment principle that a good investment is one that you think will perform better (or less badly) than the market does. However, be very careful about coming to such a conclusion. Private investors tend to be more optimistic than market investors. Poorly performing companies rarely improve. At best they get taken over for a low valuation, which is bad news for the company's shareholders.

ROCE can be considered separately for each subsidiary of a company. A low ROCE in a subsidiary indicates that it could be a candidate for a sell-off, unless the ROCE has been kept artificially low.

Variations on ROCE

Return on average capital employed (ROACE)

Return on average capital employed (ROACE) uses the same formula as that for ROCE but replaces net capital employed (NCE) with the average of the NCE at the start of the year and NCE at the end of the year. The two figures are added and the answer divided by 2.

```
Average capital employed = (NCE at year start + NCE at
                                              year end) ÷ 2

Return on average capital employed = (profit before
  interest and tax ÷ average capital employed) x 100
```

ROACE is sometimes regarded as giving a more accurate figure than ROCE, as it is a closer indication of the actual capital in use during the period than is given simply by using the figure at the end of the period.

In practice, ROACE has little else to commend it. In most businesses, there is little change in NCE from one year to the next, except a small growth in a healthy business.

Also, investors do not need to be overly concerned with finding a highly accurate figure for the ROCE and ROACE of a company. You are concerned with whether ROCE is a big number and if it is greater than the cost of capital. Knowing this information to one more decimal place is unlikely to affect any investment decision.

ROCE on trading activities

ROCE on trading activities excludes returns from non-trading activities. It excludes minority interests and government grants. This helps to identify where the returns are being earned. However, its use is limited as the investor is investing in the whole company.

ROCE excluding cash

ROCE excluding cash is a version of ROCE that nets off cash against any overdraft. This is likely to be of consequence if both the cash and overdraft amounts are significant – a situation that itself would require some explanation. In practice, this is only justified where the cash and overdraft is with the same bank and the bank calculates the overdraft interest on the net balance.

2.4
Return On Equity (ROE)

Definition

```
Return on equity = (net profit attributable to
                    shareholders ÷ equity) x 100
```

Return on equity is often abbreviated to ROE.

Net profit attributable to shareholders is the net profit after deduction of interest, tax and all other items except dividends (paid and payable). This figure is the amount available to the shareholders.

Equity in this context means the value of assets which may be regarded as owned by the shareholders. This figure is sometimes called shareholders' funds, shareholders' equity or net assets.

Shareholders' equity is calculated as follows:

```
Shareholders' equity = fixed assets + current assets -
current liabilities - long-term creditors - provisions
```

This figure for equity includes all purchased goodwill and other intangible assets. In some cases, an investor is justified in writing back goodwill that the company has written off in its accounts.

As equity is the denominator in the fraction, the larger the figure we use for equity, the smaller will be the answer. As purchased goodwill can be a relatively large figure, its addition is essential in calculating a realistic ROE.

Understanding return on equity

ROE measures the rate of profit earned by the directors for the shareholders. As such, it is a basic accounting ratio for investors.

All profit earned by a company is ultimately for the benefit of the shareholders. It is either provided immediately as dividends or provided later in the form of retained profit which enhances the capital value of the shares and allows future profits to be earned. There is always the possibility that retained profit could be squandered, but that is less likely from a management which has established a track record of effective use of capital.

How to use ROE as an investor

In general, the higher the ROE, the better it is for investors. A high figure (perhaps 15% or more for a public company and 20% for a private company) indicates a good investment prospect. Against this, the price you will have to pay for the company has probably already been factored into the good ROE.

ROE must always be considered according to the nature of the company's business. Those businesses that are primarily people-based, such as software companies and employment agencies, can have a high ROE simply because their equity base is so low. This applies equally to companies that need few assets or where their value-added is high. Conversely, companies with a heavy asset requirement, such as utilities and engineering, can indicate a lower ROE.

An investor can reasonably invest in companies with either a high or low ROE, but needs to be clear as to the reason for investment.

For a high ROE company, the investor must be satisfied that the high returns are sustainable and have not been overvalued when being factored into the share price.

For a low ROE company, the investor must see the company as a high-risk investment. This can be justified if the investor has good reason to believe that the assets are undervalued or there is a possibility of a good recovery. This could make the company a good investment if you also have reason to believe that such factors have not been fully reflected in the share price.

Variations on ROE

Return on average equity (ROAE)

Return on average equity (ROAE) is the same calculation as ROE, but replaces *equity* with *average equity*. This is the average of the shareholders' equity at the start and end of the accounting period.

This variation reflects the fact that the equity used varies during the year. ROAE is therefore more accurate than ROE. In practice, the variation is usually small and the additional accuracy adds little to the use of the ratio in decision making.

2.5
Premium to Asset Value (PAV)

Definition

```
Premium to asset value = ((share price ÷ net asset value)
                                            x 100) - 100
```

PAV is the usual abbreviation for premium to asset value. If the figure is negative, the figure is referred to as **discount to asset value.**

Share price is taken from the *Financial Times* or similar list of share prices.

Net asset value is sometimes called the **net tangible asset value.** These terms are abbreviated as either NAV or NTA, but have the same meaning. Net asset value can be difficult to calculate, as the relevant numbers are not always obvious in the financial statements.

Net asset value is calculated as:

```
(shareholders' funds - goodwill) ÷ number of shares in
                                                  issue
```

Shareholders' funds is the same as the figure for **equity** used in ROE, as explained above. It can usually be read straight from the balance sheet.

Goodwill refers only to purchased goodwill. This is an intangible asset which is either identified separately on the balance sheet or included with intangible assets or fixed assets. Many companies have no purchased goodwill on the balance sheet, so you should not be worried if you cannot find it.

Number of shares in issue refers to the number at the *end* of the accounting period. You must not use the average (as is the case for EPS, mentioned in Chapter 1). You are calculating the PAV at the end of the accounting period and so must use the number of shares in issue at the end.

Understanding PAV

PAV is a measure of value. It reflects what the market thinks of the share. It does this by ascribing a value to the share and comparing that with the actual share price.

A premium indicates a positive view of a company, probably formed on the basis of what is seen as good performance. A discount indicates a negative view of a company, probably formed on the basis of what is seen as poor performance.

How to use PAV as an investor

As a measure of value, PAV is vulnerable to the vagaries of the different systems of valuation. This means that PAV is of limited use where a company has significant property assets, particularly if they have not been revalued recently.

PAV is a useful measure for companies where assets are carefully valued. The two obvious examples are property companies and investment trusts, whose entire businesses are based on accurate valuations. PAV is also useful for all service companies.

Net asset value (NAV) can differ significantly from the value shown in the balance sheet. If using PAV, the investor should investigate such variance.

Where there is a significant difference between the NAV you have calculated and the figure for NAV given on the balance sheet this often means that the asset is significantly undervalued. Companies can often have asset values locked away because of the management style. This commonly happens in family companies. A new management, perhaps less sentimental, may realise that long-held assets are better sold or used differently. Any indication of unlocked value means that the company could be ripe for a takeover, demerger or spin-off. This is usually to the investor's advantage.

A company with a positive PAV is not automatically a good investment just as a company operating with a discount to asset value is not automatically a bad investment. PAV is a means of establishing the value of a business as seen by the market. The extent to which the company is a good investment depends on how far your view is more or less optimistic than the market view.

PAV is used by analysts for sophisticated analysis of share prices. It is doubtful if the private investor needs to be concerned with PAV.

2.6
Internal Rate of Return (IRR)

Definition

IRR is the overall rate of return from more than one variable.

This ratio cannot be calculated at all. Although a formula can be constructed, it will be found that somewhere it contains something like:

$$y = a^r + b^r$$

where r is the internal rate of return. There is no known way in algebra to make r the subject of the formula.

Instead, the answer is determined by a mathematical process known as **iteration**. This basically involves guessing at an answer and then increasing it or decreasing it until the right answer is found. The process can be done using pen and paper, but can easily take half an hour. The process can be simplified using a computer.

The Microsoft Excel spreadsheet has an =*XIRR* function which performs the calculation from data. Financial calculators can also calculate IRR. There are also many free IRR calculators listed on the web, though none of them are especially user-friendly.

All these functions require a list of inflows (positive numbers) and outflows (negative numbers) against dates. There must be at least one inflow and one outflow.

An example is an investment of £100,000 which pays £30,000 one year later and on each of the next three years. The total return is £120,000, which is a 20% return over four years. The IRR is 0.077138 or 7.7138%.

Understanding the internal rate of return

The IRR is used as a means of making a comparison between different types of investment on the same basis. IRR is also used as a tool of management accounting.

IRR not only allows shares to be compared for companies of widely differently sizes and industries, it also allows the return on shares to be compared with the returns on financial derivatives, government bonds and gilts, and other forms of investment of any kind whatsoever. If you buy an oil painting for £25,000 and sell it ten years later for £60,000, you can work out the IRR on the oil painting – it is 9.1%.

The IRR is a rate of compound interest that indicates the overall return for an investment. In effect, it expresses the earning power of the investment in the terms of a deposit account at a bank or building society.

An IRR of, say, 8% means that an investment is worth 1.08 times as much after one year. After two years, the investment is worth 1.08 x 1.08 times as much. This is 1.1664. For longer periods, the IRR can be calculated using the button marked x^y on a scientific calculator.

To find the value of 8% over, say, ten years, you multiply the original sum (the capital) by 1.08^{10}. This gives 2.159. This means that £100 invested at 8% for ten years is now worth £215.90. In other words, it has earned £115.90 interest.

Because the mathematics can be difficult to understand and calculate, it is useful to know the **rule of 72**. This states that if you divide 72 by a percentage interest rate, the answer is the number of years it will take to double your money. For 8%, this answer gives 9. Obviously this is an approximation, but it is a remarkably accurate one.

Using the internal rate of return as an investor

The investor uses IRR as a simple means of determining the return from shares when compared with investments of any other kind.

Considering risk when investing in start-ups

For the investor, the additional element of **risk** must be factored in. If you invest in small companies or start-ups, there is a high risk of failure when you will lose your entire investment. In certain trades, such as building, the annual failure rate can be as high as one-in-four.

Suppose an investor buys shares to the value of £1000 in four start-up companies. After a year, one has done well and doubled in value, the second has earned a modest 10%, the third has neither gained nor lost and the fourth has gone bust.

Your investments after one year are shown in Table 2.

Table 2 – Example of investments after one year in four companies with varying performances

Company	Value at start of year	What happened	Value at end of year
A	£1000	Doubled in value	£2000
B	£1000	Gained 10%	£1100
C	£1000	Stayed as was	£1000
D	£1000	Went bust	£0
Total	£4000		£4100

One company has done spectacularly well and that is the one that the investor will be bragging about down the pub. However, overall, the return on the investment is a trifling £100 on £4000, or 2.5%. The one company that went bust has dragged down the whole portfolio. If this company had at least retained its original value, the overall return for the portfolio would have been 27.5%.

To compensate for risk, an investor should look for much higher returns from start-ups and high-risk businesses. Typically, an investor should be looking for at least 20% and usually 30% or more. This may seem a very greedy rate, but risky investments justify a much higher premium.

2.7
Return On Assets (ROA)

Definition

```
Return on assets = (net profit ÷ net assets) x 100
```

Net profit is profit before tax and dividends.

Net assets is the total of all fixed assets (less depreciation) plus current assets, minus current liabilities.

Understanding return on assets

ROA is a simple formula widely used by banks and lenders, though it is of limited use to investors.

The ROA is a percentage which represents the return the company is itself making on what it owns. If a company has £20 million worth of assets and makes a net profit of £1 million, its ROA is just 5%. This is a poor return. The company could cease trading and simply invest its £20 million and get a better return without the effort. This assumes that the assets are saleable for their balance sheet value, which will often not be the case for fixed assets.

How to use ROA as an investor

ROA is not a particularly important ratio for investors, though its simplicity partly compensates for its limitations. There are three principle ways the ROA can be used by investors.

1. The first use of ROA is to *plot a trend over several years*. A declining ROA could indicate problems and so needs investigation. As with most adverse trends, there may be a valid reason for such a decline, but the investor must be satisfied on this. A company that moves into more long-term work could see a declining ROA even though its trading position is improving.

It is worth noting that a growing ROA does not necessarily indicate a healthy company. The company may have disposed of assets needed for future trade. This will have a short-term positive effect on ROA, but lead to long-term decline.

2. The second use of ROA is to *look at the company the way that its bank does*. Banks will generally expect to see an ROA of at least twice the rate offered from safe investments, and one which is either steady or growing or fluctuating slightly. Otherwise, the ROA could indicate that the bank may get concerned and either withdraw funding or increase its rate for providing finance.

3. The third use of ROA is to *see what profit is available*. In our example, the company has earned just 5% ROA. As some of that profit is needed to fund the company, the ROA can be viewed as the maximum return available for shareholders. This does not mean that the shareholder's return will be less than 5%, as the shareholder's return is based on the price paid for the share, not on the value of the share of the company's assets. A company with a poor ROA could still be a good investment if the shares were bought cheaply enough.

Variations on ROA

Turnover per employee is sometimes used as a measure of efficiency. The workforce is an asset, though an inflexible one. It is easier to switch off a machine for a week than to lay off a worker for a week. Turnover per employee is particularly valuable when the workforce is the main asset, such as in service industries.

2.8
Dividend Payout Ratio

Definition

```
Dividend payout ratio = dividend per share ÷ earnings per
                                                      share
```

Dividend per share is the total of the year's dividends payable for owning one share. If a company pays an interim and a final dividend, these must be added. The amount included is the amount that is actually received by the shareholder. No adjustment should be made for tax.

Earnings per share is calculated as explained in section 1.1.

Understanding dividend payout ratio

The dividend payout ratio measures how far policy relates to performance. The directors decide how much to pay the shareholders and this policy decision is usually influenced only in part by the company's performance. Most directors adopt a policy of trying to keep dividends at around the same level or aim to slowly increase them from year-to-year. Profits of good years are squirrelled away (quite legally) to compensate for the lean years.

The dividend payout ratio measures how much of the available profit is passed to the shareholders that year, as against the amount that the company retains for its future needs. If the earnings per share is 50p and the company pays 20p in dividends, the dividend payout ratio is 0.4.

There is no right answer for this ratio. Somewhere around 0.5 is usually acceptable, but there are many variables than can justify a significantly higher or lower ratio. As profits from another year may be used to fund a dividend, it is possible for this ratio to exceed 1.

How to use the dividend payout ratio as an investor

This ratio tells the investor how much of that year's profit has been distributed to shareholders rather than retained for the company's future needs. Ultimately all profits earned should benefit the shareholder, either in terms of dividend or in terms of capital growth and future profits. This ratio is therefore more concerned with the timing of the return than its amount.

An investor who is looking for an income stream will tend to favour a higher ratio, whereas a long-term investor looking for capital growth may favour a lower ratio.

An investor should be concerned if the ratio is too high, particularly for consecutive years. This could indicate an unsustainable dividend policy which restricts the company's ability to earn future profits.

Variations on the dividend payout ratio

Retained earning ratio looks at the same data from the opposite perspective of how much the company is keeping for its future needs. In the example above, the retained profit ratio is 0.6. The retained profit ratio and dividend payout ratio will always add up to 1.

3

Dividend Cover

3.1
Dividend Cover

Definition

```
Dividend cover = earnings per share ÷ dividend per share
```

Earnings per shares (EPS) is calculated as explained in Chapter 1.

Dividend per share (DPS) is determined as explained in Chapter 2.

Understanding dividend cover

Dividend cover measures how sustainable a company's dividend is.

Suppose a share has an EPS of £1.50 and pays a dividend of 50p. This gives a dividend cover of 3. It means that the EPS is enough to pay that year's dividend three times. This is probably a healthy situation. It means that the company is retaining two-thirds of its profits to maintain and expand its business.

Chapter 2 explains that companies often want to maintain their dividend record by paying a constant rate of dividend from one year to the next. The dividends in poor years may be topped up from profits kept from future years.

This is fine if the level of profits can sustain the dividend record over time. A problem arises if the profits fall and the directors take too optimistic a view about how likely they are to recover. This is quite a common occurrence.

In our example, suppose in the following year the share has an EPS of only 40p but the directors decide still to pay a dividend of 50p. The dividend cover is 0.8. This means that not only has the company not retained any profit that year, but it has had to use its reserves of cash to pay part of the dividend.

> **Any dividend cover below 1 is a warning sign.**

If business picks up in the third year, it probably does not matter much that the dividend cover was 0.8 in the second year. But suppose the third year's EPS is only 25p, yet the directors are over-optimistic and once again decide to pay a 50p dividend. The dividend cover is now just 0.5. Such a policy quickly becomes unsustainable.

How to use dividend cover as an investor

An investor is likely to consider the dividend cover when looking for a long-term steady income from shares.

For short-term holdings, you need only consider the dividend and likely capital growth for the period. If you are less concerned about having a steady income, you will monitor the share frequently or consider a volatility ratio (as explained in Chapter 9). If you are looking wholly or mainly for capital growth, you will be unconcerned about dividend anyway.

An investor should always consider the dividend cover with the **dividend yield**. A yield of 5% from a share with a dividend cover of 1.8 may provide a better sustained return than a yield of 6% from a share with a dividend cover of 1.2.

In general, the higher the dividend cover the better for a shareholder looking for continuing income. This is subject to such dividend cover being sustainable.

If the investor is looking for **capital growth** rather than regular income, the dividend cover is considered from the opposite perspective. Such an investor would look for a low dividend cover, again provided that such cover was sustainable.

4

Margins

4.1
Gross Margin and Net Margin

Definitions:

```
Gross margin = (gross profit x 100) ÷ sales revenue

Net margin = (net profit x 100) ÷ sales revenue
```

The profit is multiplied by 100 to convert a decimal into a percentage.

Gross profit is the amount of profit a company has earned before deducting its overheads (or expenses).

Net profit is the amount of profit a company has earned after deducting its overheads. This figure is before any deduction for tax or dividends to ordinary shareholders. It is after payment of dividends to preference shareholders and after any other form of payment for debt equity or borrowing.

A simplified set of company accounts is shown in Table 3.

Table 3 – A simplified set of company accounts

	Amount (£ 000s)
Sales revenue	25,000
Less cost of sales	- 12,000
Gross profit	13,000
Less overheads	- 6000
Net profit	7000

Suppose these are the accounts of a (small) supermarket. We are saying that customers spent £25 million in the year, buying goods that the supermarket had bought for £12 million. Of the £13 million gross profit, the supermarket spent £6 million on overheads such as staff wages, insurance, rates, cleaning, electricity, shelving, marketing and so on.

This gives it a net profit of £7 million. Tax is calculated on this figure (after some adjustments). The directors then decide how much of what is left should be paid as a dividend and how much should be retained for future use by the company.

Sales revenue is the income from business. The figure is the actual amount charged to customers. For a supermarket, this is likely to be the amount actually paid at the till. For most other businesses, it is the amount invoiced, even though some of the invoices have not yet been paid (of which some may never be paid).

If the company charges VAT on its supplies, the sales revenue figure excludes the VAT. This is regardless of whether or not the company may claim this back as input tax from HMRC.

Sales revenue is sometimes called *turnover*, *revenue* or *sales*. All these terms mean the same.

Sales revenue includes income from all trading sources. So a supermarket may include interest on investments and rent from unused property in addition to sales of household products.

Understanding profit margins

With profit margins we have moved from investment ratios to a pure accountancy ratio. Profit margins indicate how well the company is trading, which is one step removed from considering whether it is a good investment.

Of the two, net profit margin is the ratio of main interest to investors. It is the net profit from which dividends are paid, and from which retained profit is taken to sustain the company.

Some companies cannot readily distinguish between gross profit and net profit. It is difficult for a bank, for example, to identify what expenses should be regarded as costs rather than expenses. Even in more obvious cases, there can be marginal considerations. Is a free carrier bag in a supermarket a cost of supplying the product or an expense of being in business?

Profit margins must refer to a **period.** Normally this is an accounting period, which is usually one year to the date of the balance sheet.

How to use profit margins as an investor

Profit margins tell you how successfully the company is trading.

What figure to look for in margins

For smaller companies, healthy gross profit margins are typically between 50% and 30% respectively. Those are the sorts of returns an investor would expect, unless there is a special factor relating to the nature of the business that justifies lower returns. Any net profit margin below 15% should usually be of concern.

Gross profit margin

Gross profit margin indicates whether the company has got its pricing structure right. The cost of sales should be directly related to revenue. If the supermarket sold 1000 tons of potatoes, it had to buy 1000 tons of potatoes.

If a company does not make a gross profit, the circumstances should be looked at very carefully. It means the company is selling products for less than it paid for them. Even for a start-up company or an established company going through a period of bleak profits, there is no justification for a **gross loss.**

Net profit margin

Net profit margin is the figure which is much more important to all users of accounts. It is easy to incur overheads. A case can always be made out for recruiting more staff, more advertising, improving the premises or buying another piece of equipment.

Although such expenditure can be cost-justified at the time, overheads have a habit of never quite delivering what is expected. If you leave expenses unwatched, they have a habit of breeding and multiplying.

Traditionally, investors were often satisfied with a net profit of 10% for an established business, with margins as low as 3% for high-volume, cash-positive businesses such as supermarkets. Only smaller high-risk companies were expected to do better, with a 30% margin often regarded as the minimum acceptable. Today, investors are likely to expect higher returns.

Some low-cost businesses, such as service companies (e.g. employment agencies and advertising agencies) can manage 50% net margins. As with most ratios, understanding the business is key to understanding the ratio.

Net profit margin as a measure of efficiency

Net profit margin is also a measure of efficiency. In the 1970s, telephones were nationalised and operated inefficiently, laden with overheads. The standard work rate for connections was for two engineers to connect two telephones in a day. Today there is competition. One operator, Virgin, has a standard of requiring *one* engineer to connect eight telephones a day. This is not a 10% efficiency improvement – it is a 700% efficiency improvement.

A high net profit margin is usually a good sign, as it may indicate effective management. A sustained high margin can indicate that the company is vulnerable to aggressive competition. Some analysts prefer slightly above average margins.

A low net profit margin should always be investigated. It may not be a bad sign, such as if the business has just expanded significantly or is operating in a high-volume, cash-positive environment. If not, a low net profit margin indicates a company that could fail if there is even a small downturn in its fortunes.

Observing trends in margins

An investor should look at the *trend* in margins. This means that you should look at margins over a period of perhaps five to ten years.

For a healthy company, these should normally be steady or slightly increasing each year. Fluctuating margins or declining margins may be indicators of problems ahead, such as growing inefficiency or heavy overheads. There may be good reasons for this, but you should satisfy yourself on this point.

Margins can also be used for **comparison** with other companies *in the same business*. In all these areas, think through what the business actually does. A software company has few costs and expenses: basically just people, an office and a few bits of equipment. A utility company has massive overheads maintaining vast networks of water mains or electricity cables. So a utility company typically has lower margins than a software company.

In making any comparison, it is important to compare like with like. Because depreciation and hire charges are matters of policy that have little effect on profit margins, analysts sometimes add these figures back to net profit when making comparisons.

Variations on gross and net margins

Operating margin

Operating margin is a variation on the gross profit margin. It strips out those elements of income which are not part of the company's main business, such as investment income and rent. It gives a more realistic view of gross margin. However, as gross margin is not that important to investors anyway, it is not usually worth calculating this ratio.

Pre-tax margin

Pre-tax margin is a variation on the net profit margin. It uses the figure for net profit before tax, so that tax is excluded from the reckoning. It is difficult to see what advantage is gained from using this ratio, as only the after-tax profit is available for distribution to shareholders.

Break-even point

Break-even point is an alternative method of considering gross profit margin. It is more likely to be used by the company itself as a management accounting tool than by an investor. Break-even point looks at the direct costs of providing the company's products or services and asks how many it must sell before covering its indirect costs or overheads. Suppose a company has overheads of £10 million. It buys or produces items at £5 each and sells them for £9. Each product makes a contribution of £4 towards the overheads, so the company needs to sell 2.5 million to break even.

The problem with this measure is that it only works properly when the company sells just one product or service. For a range of products, some apportionment of overheads is necessary. The investor only needs to understand break-even to the extent that it is mentioned in a narrative report.

4.2
Overheads to Turnover

Definition:

```
Overheads to turnover = (overheads ÷ turnover) x 100
```

Overheads are all the expenses or indirect costs of the company. These are the items listed between gross profit and net profit in the profit and loss account.

Turnover is the figure for sales or revenue. It is usually the first figure quoted in the profit and loss account.

Both of these figures can be determined in different ways, depending on what is included. As this ratio is most useful for detecting trends, the exact scope of what is included is not important, provided that all such ratios are calculated on the same basis.

Understanding overheads to turnover

This ratio provides a simple measure of how far the company has its overheads under control. By itself, the ratio means little; its most effective use is to determine trends.

As with most trends, there is no simple correlation between cause and effect. A gradual deterioration in this ratio could indicate that overheads are not properly under control. However, a sudden deterioration could indicate a significant increase in overheads which may be a good sign of the company taking appropriate steps to secure its future. Equally, it could indicate a significant loss of control. A sharp drop in this ratio is almost certainly a bad sign if it is not promptly reversed.

For a small business, this ratio should gradually decline as the business grows. This is a combination of two factors. First, there is the greater utilisation of the trading capacity created for the business, such as greater use of the stock room and invoicing systems. Second, businesses should always find ways to economise once they are trading.

Banks and other lenders often use this ratio in making lending decisions to smaller businesses. A failure to see a gradual decrease in the ratio could indicate that the company will have difficulties in borrowing funds.

Variations on overheads to turnover

Expense ratio uses the same principle as overheads to turnover but concentrates on a particular item of expenditure. An investor may be concerned about how much a company is spending on consultants, hire fees, legal costs, security or almost any other overhead. In practice, an investor is likely to use the expense ratio after being concerned about the overheads to turnover ratio.

5

Gearing

5.1
Gearing Ratio

Definition

```
Gearing = ((Total borrowings - cash) x 100) ÷ shareholders'
                                                      funds
```

Gearing is a term borrowed from engineering.

The diagram above shows that, if you have two adjacent cogs, turning the smaller one will rotate the larger one. The greater the difference, the more large rotations you get from rotating the small wheel. This is the principle of gears on cars and bicycles, where higher gearing is used for higher speeds.

In accounting, gearing similarly means the ratio of output to input in terms of financial return to the ordinary shareholder as measured by EPS (explained in Chapter 1).

Total borrowings means all forms of debt equity. This includes preference shares, loan stock and loan notes. It includes loans and bank overdrafts and any other form of borrowing. In short, it is any arrangement where a company gets money for its business other than as ordinary shares or earning profit.

Cash means banknotes and coins on the premises, amounts in the bank and any other form of currency or equivalent which is available for immediate spending.

Shareholders' funds are that part of the business which is collectively owned by the shareholders. This is the total of fixed assets (after depreciation) and current assets. From this you subtract current liabilities, long-term creditors and provisions.

Understanding gearing

Gearing is the ratio between equity funding and debt funding. A highly geared company is one where the company has high levels of debt funding (borrowing) in relation to its share value. Note that a company must always have some equity funding, but need not have any debt funding. A company with no debt funding is said to be ungeared.

When a company needs money to start its business or to expand its business, it has two basic choices. It can issue shares or it can borrow money.

The financial markets have developed a bewildering array of financial instruments by which a company may acquire funds. Financial Reporting Standard FRS 4 has an entire section listing them and explaining what they are. They include such exotic instruments as convertible debt with a premium put option, repackaged perpetual debt and stepped interest bonds.

All of these instruments are variations on one of two themes, or a combination of both. A company either issues shares or borrows money. If it issues shares, it sells part of itself. This is what contestants do on *Dragons' Den*. If someone sells 30% of their business for £100,000, that means that the owner has £100,000 on which no interest is payable, but it means that the dragon is entitled to 30% of the profits of the business for evermore, or until the 30% stake in the business is sold.

An alternative is to borrow money. Interest must be paid whatever the profits (usually), but the original owner keeps all the profits.

All this is best explained by a simple example.

Example: financing a business

Suppose a company needs £1 million to start a business. It considers various mixes of equity funding (ordinary shares of £1 each) and debt funding (preference shares carrying 5% interest). It considers four amounts of preference shares:

- zero (ungeared)
- £200,000 (low geared)
- £500,000 (medium geared)
- £900,000 (high geared)

As the preference shares carry 5% interest it means that the company must pay interest each year of zero, £10,000, £25,000 and £45,000 respectively, regardless of profits. The remainder of the £1 million capital is in the form of ordinary shares. So if the option of low gearing is taken and £200,000 is raised through the sale of preference shares, the remainder of the £1 million (£800,000) will be raised through the sale of ordinary shares.

For each of these four choices, we now look to see what happens when the company makes a profit of:

- £30,000 (low profit)
- £45,000 (medium profit)
- £100,000 (high profit)
- £300,000 (very high profit)

The capital structure is set out in Table 4.

Table 4 – Capital structure

Gearing	Ungeared	Low geared	Medium geared	High geared
Preference shares	zero	£200,000	£500,000	£900,000
Interest payable (at 5%)	zero	£10,000	£25,000	£45,000
Ordinary shares (at £1 each)	1,000,000	800,000	500,000	100,000

We now look to see what happens to the EPS (explained in Chapter 1) for an ordinary share for each profit level at each level of gearing (Table 5).

Table 5 – How EPS is affected by different levels of gearing

	Ungeared	Low geared	Medium geared	High geared
Low profit	30,000	30,000	30,000	30,000
Interest payable	zero	10,000	25,000	45,000
Profit - interest	30,000	20,000	5000	(15,000)
EPS	**3p**	**2.5p**	**1p**	**–15p**
Medium profit	45,000	45,000	45,000	45,000
Interest payable	zero	10,000	25,000	45,000
Profit - interest	45,000	35,000	20,000	zero
EPS	**4.5p**	**4.375p**	**4p**	**0p**
High profit	100,000	100,000	100,000	100,000
Interest payable	zero	10,000	25,000	45,000
Profit - interest	100,000	90,000	75,000	55,000
EPS	**10p**	**11.25p**	**15p**	**55p**
Very high profit	**300,000**	**300,000**	**300,000**	**300,000**
Interest payable	zero	10,000	25,000	45,000
Profit - interest	300,000	290,000	275,000	255,000
EPS	**30p**	**36.25p**	**55p**	**255p**

For convenience, we extract the EPS figures from the above calculations (Table 6).

Table 6 – EPS at different levels of gearing

	Ungeared	Low geared	Medium geared	High geared
Low profit	3p	2.5p	1p	-15p
Medium profit	4.5p	4.375p	4p	0p
High profit	10p	11.25p	15p	55p
Very high profit	30p	36.25p	55p	255p

If we plot these figures on a chart, they appear as in Chart 1.

Chart 1: Different levels of EPS based upon varying amounts of gearing

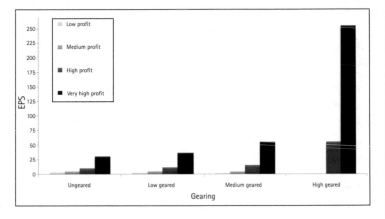

The points to note are:

- In good years, gearing makes EPS better and in bad years gearing makes EPS worse.
- High gearing has a dramatic effect on EPS – hence the term gearing.
- High gearing can turn a profit into a loss for ordinary shareholders when profits are low.
- Low levels of gearing have a small effect on the EPS.

Gearing has a magnifying effect on EPS.

How to use gearing as an investor

Gearing in established businesses and new businesses

The first question any investor should ask is why there is gearing at all, particularly for an **established company**.

If the company is consistently making profits, where are they? If a company is consistently trading at a net profit, **cash** will be pouring into its bank accounts. Rates of corporation tax in recent years have never been above 30%, so at least 70% of that money is available to the company. Some of that is paid in dividends and some is used to fund further expansion.

When a company can provide enough funding from profits for development, that is known as **organic growth**. An investor should always be sceptical about any need for inorganic growth from an established company. High gearing is often needed because the company has been irresponsible in its use of funds, either in paying too much dividend, by buying other businesses or through incurring overheads that are not cost-justified.

For a **new business**, the position is different. A company is often formed with a share capital of just £2 and with the real working capital provided by loans from the directors of perhaps £10,000. This gives a gearing ratio, not of the high figure of 9:1 (the highest in our example), but of 5001:1. This is a meaninglessly high figure. Gearing is often inappropriate as a consideration in a new business.

As with all indicators, gearing may be used to **compare** similar companies in the same business that are of a similar size and age.

How high gearing should be interpreted

Because of the vagaries of **accounting practice**, a high gearing ratio may not be a reliable indicator. A healthy company may have a high gearing ratio because assets are undervalued. This is usually because buildings have not been valued recently or because depreciation rates are high.

Bankers and lenders often like to see the gearing ratio no higher than 50%. This means that the amount borrowed is no more (and preferably less) than the shareholders' funds. If the gearing ratio is above 50%, the investor may need to consider whether the company is likely to be able to acquire necessary loans at a reasonable rate.

Where there genuinely is high gearing, this should be considered with the company's **volatility** (explained in Chapter 9). The lower the volatility, the more easily a company can survive with high gearing.

Gearing and the nature of debt equity

The **nature of debt equity** should always be considered. As against ordinary loans, cumulative preference shares are preferable and convertible preference shares less preferable to the ordinary shareholder.

A **cumulative preference share** means that if the company cannot pay the interest one year, it is rolled over to be paid in a future year. This avoids the need for the company to pay out cash it may desperately need to recover. In contrast, a **convertible preference share** gives its holder the best of both worlds. While profits are low, he can receive a guaranteed rate, and when profits improve he can convert them to ordinary shares and share profits on the same terms as other ordinary shareholders who suffered when profits were low.

Some forms of debt equity have **variable interest rates**. They may be linked to the Retail Prices Index (general inflation) or to the bank base rate. For such instruments, the risks of high gearing are compounded by the high risk of increases in these rates. A company could find itself in the position that high interest rates reduce sales while increasing its borrowing costs, meaning that one cause has two adverse effects.

A high risk of debt equity is where the rate is linked to a **credit rating**. If the company's credit rating is reduced, the interest rate goes up, often significantly. Perhaps the highest risk is the **junk bond** where money is lent at a high interest rate. It is a do-or-die financial instrument. If the company prospers it can pay the high interest rate, failing which, the company goes bust. It is possible for an investor still to make money from such companies, but it requires specialist investment knowledge.

High gearing as a positive for shareholders

While high gearing is always a warning sign to investors, it can be an **advantage** to shareholders.

If the company reports **rising profits**, high gearing has the effect of magnifying the benefit to the shareholders.

High gearing also introduces an element of gambling into the investment and can therefore appeal to those who are able to take such risks.

The concept of **risk and reward** states that the greater the risk, the greater the reward offered. Suppose a company has a 10% chance of growing 30-fold over four years and a 90% chance of becoming worthless. That is not a share for the cautious investor. However, if you invest in ten such companies, the probability is that one company will succeed and nine companies will fail. The one success gives a handsome overall return of 210%. This is not guaranteed, as there is still a 34.9% chance that all ten companies will fail. However the concept means that the more you can diversify, the lower is the risk while maintaining the overall reward, and this reward will be higher than obtainable from a safer investment.

High gearing can also appeal to investors who fancy a **gamble**. However, such investors are more likely to buy options or futures, as the up-front investment is lower and the pay-back periods shorter.

5.2
Interest Cover

Definition

```
Interest cover = (pre-tax profit + interest paid) ÷ interest
                                                        paid
```

Pre-tax profit and **interest paid** are both shown in the profit and loss account.

Interest paid should be a net figure, calculated by subtracting any interest received.

Understanding interest cover

Interest cover is a similar ratio to dividend cover (mentioned in Chapter 3). Interest cover indicates how many times the company could afford to pay the net interest on its borrowings.

While the principle and calculation are similar to dividend cover, it represents something completely different. Dividend is a matter of *policy*, the company could always simply reduce or cancel the dividend. The shareholders may not be pleased, but it would protect the company. Interest is (usually) payable regardless of profits. If the figure is low, say 3 or less, this could indicate that the company is struggling to meet its liabilities. This could have some serious implications for the company's profitability and survival.

Interest cover is only relevant when a company has significant borrowings. If a company has a cash balance which exceeds its borrowings, there is no need to calculate this ratio.

Using interest cover as an investor

To the investor, interest cover is a warning signal, both of profitability and survival.

The first indication that can be drawn from interest cover is of **interest sensitivity**. Interest cover can indicate how vulnerable the company is to changes in interest rates. In 2009, interest rates reached 0.5% – the lowest levels in recorded history. In May 1988, by contrast, the base rate was 7.5%. One year later in May 1989, it had almost doubled to 14%. Any company with significant loans linked to the base rate was badly hit in this situation.

Interest cover similarly indicates the ability of the company to survive **poor trading**. In this, the interest cover is ancillary to the profit margins.

High interest cover indicates high **gearing**, which has the effect of magnifying profits and losses for the shareholder.

If the borrowings take the form of bonds, there is a further rate of **interest covenants**. These are policies included in the terms of the bond issue. Bonds sometimes include a covenant which imposes penalties or increases the interest rate if the interest cover falls below a specified figure. Bond holders and other lenders often monitor interest cover closely for this reason. The lenders regard their loans as having become much more risky, and therefore seek additional interest to compensate. Such an eventuality has the consequence of making a bad situation much worse for the shareholders.

The terms of any such covenants should be disclosed in the notes to the accounts. This is likely to be buried in a mass of text and numbers after the main accounts. The profit and loss account, and probably the balance sheet also, will have a number under the heading *Notes to the Accounts*. This refers to a later page where the terms of all such bonds are set out. The investor should make a value judgment on whether the terms are likely to reduce the available profits for dividends, or even to threaten the ability of the company to survive. A sensible lender is unlikely to let a borrower go bust if the consequence is that the loans will be unpaid. However, a lender could be willing to let the company get into serious trouble before bailing it out on terms which are advantageous to the lender and disadvantageous to shareholders.

Interest cover indicates a risk which may arise from a **price war**. Company accounts are public documents that are read by competitors as well as investors. In management terms, a price war is usually seen as a quick route to collective financial suicide. However, companies still engage in price wars, particularly if they believe that it will provide a quick kill of their competitors. A cash-rich competitor may well be willing to wage a price war to increase the strain on a competitor, particularly if there is scope for then buying the competitor.

6

Solvency Ratios

6.1
Acid Test

Definition

```
Acid test = (current assets - stock) ÷ current
                                       liabilities
```

Acid test is sometimes called the **acid test ratio, acid ratio, liquidity ratio** or **quick ratio**. Occasionally it is referred to as the **current ratio**, but that term is better reserved for a different ratio explained below.

The term comes from the California Gold Rush of the 1850s when it was often difficult to distinguish valuable gold from worthless iron pyrites. A simple test was to use nitric acid, which was cheap and readily available. A drop of acid would quickly react with iron pyrites but gold would be unaffected. From this, the term was extended to any quick test to check provenance.

Current assets are cash, its equivalents and those things that will become cash. Typically current assets includes debtors, prepayments and stock, though the last of these is excluded for the acid test. Debtors are sometimes called debts, accounts receivable or receivables. Sometimes short-term investments which can readily be converted into cash are also included.

Stock comprises those items which the company holds with a view to selling, either as they are or after some process, such as manufacture, assembly or packaging. The word **inventory** is sometimes used, as the word stock also means a form of equity capital.

Current assets minus stock is sometimes called **quick assets** because these can be quickly turned into cash, unlike stock which has to be sold.

Current liabilities are the opposite of current assets; the company is obliged to pay money in the next 12 months as a result of an event which has already happened. In modern accounting parlance, this now usually appears on the balance sheet as **creditors due within one year.** Sometimes the figure is referred to simply as **creditors.** Sums due in more than 12 months (such as deferred tax and loans) are not included. Current liabilities comprises creditors (amounts owed to suppliers and others) plus accruals, which is usually a small figure.

Understanding the acid test

The acid test is a solvency ratio. This measures how able the company is to continue trading in the foreseeable future. We are no longer looking at how much return you will receive on your investment but whether you will continue to receive any return at all.

It is first necessary to understand the **going concern concept.** By law, every company must prepare its accounts under this concept unless it explicitly states otherwise. Financial Reporting Standard FRS 18 paragraph 21 states:

> An entity should prepare its financial statements on a going concern basis, unless:
>
> (a) the entity is being liquidated or has ceased trading, or
>
> (b) the directors have no realistic alternative but to liquidate the entity or to cease trading, in which circumstances the entity may prepare its financial statements on a basis other than that of a going concern.

In other words, you may assume that a company expects to continue trading for the foreseeable future unless the accounts specifically state otherwise. If the going concern is not used this will be expressly stated, usually in Note 1 to the accounts.

The alternative to the going concern concept is usually **forced realisation**. This usually means that assets are worth less and demands on cash flow are much greater.

Directors tend to be more optimistic than auditors, so it is always worth looking at the end of their report. However, even reading the auditor's caution may not be enough. Of companies that fail, only about half have any such qualification in their last accounts.

The acid test looks to see if the balance between assets and liabilities is reasonable. Does the company have enough to pay its creditors?

How to use the acid test as an investor

The **traditional yardstick** is that any acid test above 1 is safe. That means that any company whose quick assets are at least as much as its current liabilities is solvent.

As with most ratios this is a good starting point, but no more. It is also necessary to look at the nature of the company's trade and thus at its **cash flow**. This is how quickly cash outflows are compensated by cash inflows.

Supermarkets and oil companies can safely trade on much lower acid tests than 1. A supermarket usually sells its goods for immediate cash (no waiting for invoices to be paid) before it has paid its supplier. This is called being **cash positive**. The most extreme example was Green Shield trading stamps (offered between 1958 and 1983). There could be such a long period between the company receiving payment from the shops and paying the suppliers for the goods for which the shop customers redeemed the stamps, that special company law was introduced for trading stamp companies.

The opposite extreme is found in construction and utilities where there are huge up-front costs and it can take years to recover these from cash inflows. Such companies are known as **cash negative**.

Where a company has a particularly positive or negative cash flow, the acid test is still useful to compare that company with other companies in a similar business.

Acid test and similar solvency ratios are of particular benefit valuing young companies (but not start-up companies) that have a normal cash flow. The acid test is also particularly useful when assessing companies that operate in niche markets.

6.2
Current Ratio

Definition

```
Current ratio = current assets ÷ current liabilities
```

Current assets are cash, its equivalents and those things that will become cash. Typically current assets include debtors, prepayments and stock, though the last of these is excluded for the acid test. Debtors are sometimes called debts, accounts receivable or receivables. Sometimes short-term investments which can readily be converted into cash are also included.

Current liabilities are the opposite of current assets; the company is obliged to pay money in the next 12 months as a result of an event which has already happened. In modern accounting parlance, this now usually appears on the balance sheet as **creditors due within one year**. Sometimes the figure is referred to simply as **creditors**. Sums due in more than 12 months (such as deferred tax and loans) are not included. Current liabilities comprises creditors (amounts owed to suppliers and others) plus accruals, which is usually a small figure.

Understanding current ratio

Current ratio is a solvency test. It is best seen as a variation of the acid test previously explained. The difference is that the current ratio does not exclude stock from current assets.

The current ratio is appropriate when the stock is readily saleable. This will apply when the product is in wide demand, such as for oil or common consumer goods as sold by a supermarket.

How to use current ratio as an investor

An investor wanting to use a solvency ratio should use either the acid test or current ratio, but not both.

If the investor decides that the stock held by the company is of a nature that it can be regarded as readily convertible to cash, i.e. it is **liquid**, then the current ratio is likely to be more appropriate than the acid test.

Otherwise the use of the current ratio is identical to the acid test.

6.3
Cash Burn

Definition

```
Cash burn = capital at start of year ÷ year's cash
                                        expenditure
```

Capital at start of year is the amount of cash (not debtors or stock) at the start of the accounting period. This may be read from the cash flow statement, not from the profit and loss account.

Year's cash expenditure is the amount of cash spent during the year. This is also taken from the cash flow statement. Cash generated from profits and interest received may be deducted from this expenditure.

Cash burn is sometimes called **burn rate**.

Understanding cash burn

Cash burn is only appropriate for a new or refinanced business which has yet to earn profits. It measures how long the finance will last.

There is no agreed definition for this formula; the definition quoted here is a very narrow one. You may, for example, wish to include debtors or even stock in the capital at the start of the year.

The initial capital is often invested, so its use also has the effect of reducing the interest earned. However, no financier provides funds to earn interest in a bank. It is more likely that the financier will agree a sum to be called down as required, such as providing £400,000 in four tranches of £100,000.

In practice, businesses start to generate small amounts of income from an early stage. This will reduce the cash burn. For example, a business may cost £100,000 a year to run and may be financed with £300,000 cash.

Its cash burn is simply £300,000 ÷ £100,000 = 3. In other words, it will run out of funds in three years.

This business generates £20,000 profit in the first year and this grows at 50% a year (which is quite possible for a new business). This could be plotted as in Table 6.

Table 6 – An example of how cash is burned in the first eight years of a business' trading

Year	Start	Cost	Start–cost	Net income	End
1	300,000	100,000	200,000	20,000	220,000
2	220,000	100,000	120,000	30,000	150,000
3	150,000	100,000	50,000	45,000	95,000
4	95,000	100,000	-5000	67,500	62,500
5	62,500	100,000	-37,500	101,250	63,750
6	63,750	100,000	-36,250	151,875	115,625
7	115,625	100,000	15,625	227,812	243,438
8	243,438	100,000	143,438	341,719	485,156

Here it can be seen that the company does survive until the net income has grown sufficiently before the cash is fully burned. The lowest point was after five years, when all but £62,500 of the cash was used. It is in year 5 that the sales have grown large enough to carry the costs.

However, this example makes some sweeping assumptions. Costs are unchanged from year-to-year and net income keeps growing at a high rate (which becomes progressively more difficult to maintain in reality).

If the company only achieved 40% growth (which is still impressive), the cash would hit a low of £18,912 after five years.

If the company only achieved 30% growth, it would go into overdraft for four years from years 5 to 8, hitting a low of -£48,343 at the end of year 7.

The above does not readily lend itself to a formula which can be solved by algebra or calculus. It is probably better to plot the figures on a spreadsheet, trying the projected rate of growth and also lower rates of growth to see what happens. The rate of growth should be stated by the company in its annual report. If the figure in the final column ever goes negative, the company is almost certainly a poor investment.

How to use cash burn as an investor

Cash burn indicates whether you should invest in the business at all.

Suppose a business has £2 million and spent £500,000 during the year. At that rate, it will have burnt through the cash in four years. If it has not started to earn sufficient profit by then, the business will either fail or have to be refinanced. Refinancing is always bad news for existing shareholders. The new shareholders will expect to receive first claim on all future profits and your holding will be worth little.

It is rarely advisable to invest in a start-up or refinanced company unless satisfied that it will earn sufficient profits before the cash runs out.

The investor should already have considered using the EV/EBITDA ratio (as explained in Chapter 1).

6.4
Defensive Interval

Definition:

```
Defensive interval = liquid assets ÷ daily operating
                                        expenses
```

Liquid assets are cash and debtors. Stock may be included, provided there is reason to believe that it is all readily and quickly saleable.

Daily operating expenses are the costs of running a business for one day. This is every expense and cost of the business. It is everything subtracted from turnover to arrive at net profit before tax and distributions. It includes interest payments to lenders and all payments to holders of preference shares, debentures and similar forms of debt finance.

Understanding defensive interval

Defensive interval measures the number of days a company could survive without any more cash coming in.

To some extent, this measure is illusory for two reasons:

1. Why would the money suddenly stop coming in? Even if the company's credit control failed completely, it would be reasonable to expect most of the invoices still to be paid, even if later than intended. If there were a complete failure of the banking system, this would affect the entire country rather than any specific company.

2. A company which faced cash flow problems should quickly take steps to alleviate the problem. Costs would be cut and new sources of income identified.

The main reason for including this interval in the book is because the UK government-backed Business Link service (www.businesslink.gov.uk) includes it as one of its three liquidity ratios. It is also quoted in a few other places, but otherwise has not established itself as an important ratio.

How to use defensive interval as an investor

In so far as this ratio serves any purpose at all, it indicates the extent to which a business is prepared for the unexpected. The Business Link website suggests that the interval should lie between 30 and 90, meaning that the company could last for between one and three months without any further receipts. Many very healthy companies manage on lower figures.

If a company has a very low defensive interval, the nature of its business should be considered. A cash-positive business could manage much more easily than a cash-negative business.

If a company has a very high defensive interval, this could indicate that the company is stockpiling cash, which may not be providing the most efficient return on its resources.

6.5
Fixed Charges Cover

Definition

```
Fixed charges cover = net profit before fixed charges ÷
                                            fixed charges
```

Fixed charges are the expenses a company must pay regardless of whether it is trading. Examples of fixed charges include:

- Rent, maintenance charges and similar property expenses.

- All forms of interest payable (regardless of whether they are long term).

- Business rates and any other property taxes.

- Lease payments and hire charges.

- Any other fixed expense which the company must pay and cannot readily cancel.

Net profit before fixed charges is net profit before tax and interest payments, plus the fixed charges as determined above.

Understanding fixed charges cover

Fixed charges cover indicates how well the company can survive a lean period. It takes all the expenses that cannot be quickly reduced and looks to see how readily the business can continue paying them.

Any figure above 1.5 generally indicates a healthy company.

This ratio is a simple but crude indicator of solvency. Fixed charges excludes staff, though staff cannot be laid off without costs such as redundancy pay and possibly the costs associated with industrial action. Utilities, such as water and electricity, often cannot be readily scaled back.

Against this, the figure looks at how well a company could survive for one year (because the ratio uses annual figures). In practice, many of the fixed costs may be cancelled within one year.

How to use fixed charges cover as an investor

Fixed charges cover is of particular interest during adverse economic conditions, such as during a recession. It is also relevant if that particular industry is experiencing trading difficulties, even though the general economy may be healthy.

During the 1990/91 recession, many property development companies failed because they had insufficient steady income (such as rent) to keep going during the lean times. This measure proved to be a reliable indicator of which companies were in difficulty and subsequently went on to fail.

7

Efficiency Ratios

7.1
Stock Turn

Definition

```
Stock turn = sales ÷ closing stock
```

Sales is the revenue from selling goods and services (as explained in Chapter 4).

Stock is the value of goods held for sale at the end of the accounting period (as explained in Chapter 6).

Understanding stock turn

Stock turn is a measure of business efficiency. The number indicates how many times the company sells a stock item during the course of an accounting period. This is sometimes expressed in the form of **stock days** (explained below). The higher the number, the more efficient is the business.

Suppose a company has sales of £100 million and closing stock of £10 million; its stock turn is 10. This means that, on average, the company will buy an item and sell it ten times during the year. Another way of looking at it is that an item takes just over a month from acquisition to sale.

This is not strictly accurate, as the sales figure includes the gross profit margin. Suppose the company spent £60 million (its **cost of sales**) buying the goods it sold for £100 million. You could then calculate the stock turn by dividing the cost of sales by the closing stock. This would give a more accurate figure of 6 for stock turn, indicating that there was an average of two months between acquisition and sale (12 months ÷ 6 = 2 months). However, dividing cost of sales by closing stock is never used in practice. As an efficiency ratio, any inefficiency in holding stock can be compensated by a greater profit margin. A management consultant may be interested in a cost of sales turn, but an investor is only interested in overall efficiency.

Stock turn is a figure which is heavily influenced by the nature of the business. At one extreme a dairy should have a very high stock turn. If a dairy product is not sold within a few days of manufacture, it deteriorates and must be discarded. At the other extreme, a book publisher or antiques shop may acquire large amounts of stock which can take years to sell.

A problem with stock turn is that it can conceal widely different figures between stock lines. For example, many supermarkets have diversified from selling mainly food into selling clothes, electrical goods and even furniture. These new product ranges typically have a much lower stock turn than food.

This ratio may only be used for companies that sell tangible goods. For banks, utilities and service companies, the ratio is meaningless. Such companies will probably still have some stock, but dividing the revenue of a bank by the value of its stationery provides a meaningless figure.

How to use stock turn as an investor

For the investor, the main use of stock turn is to detect trends within the company. Stock turn has little value considered on its own or as a comparator with similar businesses.

A constant or slightly upward trend indicates that the company is becoming more efficient. A downward trend could indicate that the company is becoming less efficient.

Variation on stock turn

We already covered one variation on stock turn above – the cost of sales turn. Another variation is **stock days**.

Stock days divides stock by sales and multiplies the answer by 365.

```
Stock days = (stock ÷ sales) x 365
```

This is a multiple of the reciprocal of stock turn and measures exactly the same aspect of efficiency. This measure is sometimes preferred as it gives an answer in the more comprehensible form of days. In our example above, the company would have a stock turn of:

(£10 million ÷ £100 million) x 365 days = 36.5 days

This means that an item of stock is, on average, held for 36.5 days before being sold. As the main value of stock turn is for detecting trends, there seems no obvious reason for preferring this variation.

7.2
Price-to-Book Value (PBV)

Definition

```
Price-to-book value (PBV) = market capitalisation ÷
                                shareholders' equity
```

Market capitalisation is the value of the company, measured by multiplying the number of shares by their current value (as explained in Chapter 1).

Shareholders' equity is the value of the business as shown by **net tangible assets** or **net assets**. This figure should appear under one of these names on the balance sheet.

There are some variations on exactly what is included in each of these figures. So, if a comparison is made between earlier years or with other companies, you must be sure that the ratios have been calculated on the same basis.

The main differences relate to minority interests, purchased goodwill and property revaluations. Probably the best option is to include property at the professional value, and investments at either cost or market value. Other items should be excluded.

This ratio is abbreviated to PBV.

Understanding price-to-book value

This ratio measures how good the current performance of the share price is in relation to the assets owned by the company. Suppose the company has 1 million shares with a current market value of £2 each, and has shareholders' equity of £1.2 million. Its market capitalisation is £2 million and its price-to-book value is 1.67. This means that the market value is 67% greater than the net assets.

PBV is sometimes seen as a quick measure of how well the company's assets are working for the shareholders.

PBV tends to be a reliable indicator only for companies which are rich in tangible assets, such as utility companies. PBV has less relevance for companies which have few tangible assets.

How to use price-to-book value as an investor

While this ratio is still encountered, it is difficult to see what it indicates that is not better indicated by another ratio.

The shareholder is not primarily bothered by how well the assets are working (for which there are more precise efficiency measures anyway), but by the overall return.

7.3
Overtrading and Undertrading

Definition

```
Overtrading = capital required ÷ capital available
```

Overtrading and **undertrading** are the same measure and are calculated in the same way.

Capital required is a subjective measure of how much capital a business needs to operate properly. It is the sum needed to acquire adequate premises, staff, fixed assets, stock and similar assets to realise the company's commercial potential.

Capital available is the total of shareholders' funds, retained profit, loan capital, directors' loans and any other form of funding for the company.

Evidence of overtrading or undertrading may also be found from other ratios (see below).

Understanding overtrading and undertrading

Overtrading and undertrading mean that the company is either over-capitalised or under-capitalised.

As *capital required* is a subjective measure, or a matter of opinion, it can be argued that this is not really an accounting ratio at all. Asking a company how much money it needs is rather like asking a child how much pocket money he or she *needs*. The other element of *capital available* can be determined exactly.

While the calculations are the same for overtrading and undertrading, their nature is different.

Overtrading is the more serious problem. It means that the company is constantly struggling to operate. Usually this means it has insufficient stock to meet orders properly and insufficient staff to look after customers and do the job properly. It will be reluctant to offer normal trade terms to customers and may be slow in paying its own debts.

Overtrading can also be detected from other ratios thus:

- *Current ratio* is likely to be very low.

- *Turnover ratios* are likely to be high.

- *Creditor days* are likely to be high (see Chapter 8).

- *Debtor days* may be low.

Undertrading is usually less serious. It means that the company has more capital than it needs. This typically takes the form of spare cash which will usually not earn the same income as the trading income; it should not do so.

Even if a company's required capital could be measured exactly, it is unlikely that any company would ever be capitalised to exactly the right level. So every company is probably overtrading or undertrading. For this reason, overtrading and (even more so) undertrading is usually only considered a problem if the difference is significant, such as an overtrading ratio above 2 or an undertrading ratio below 0.75.

How to use overtrading and undertrading as an investor

An investor should always be concerned about a company that appears to be overtrading.

First, the investor should ask why the company cannot obtain adequate finance. If it is a well-run profitable company with good prospects, why are banks and investors not willing to provide the capital? At best, this indicates a problem with management.

Second, an overtrading company is likely to be continually encountering problems in its everyday work. It will be annoying its customers and suppliers, and never meeting its proper potential.

An undertrading company is of much less concern to the investor. At worst, it means that the company is not properly using its assets and so may be earning a lower return than if the assets were more effectively used. An investor should also consider what the company intends to do with any cash pile. It has been known for companies to fritter away cash resources acquiring unprofitable subsidiaries.

7.4
Item Comparison

Definition

```
Item comparison = Item in accounts for current year ÷
                          Same item for previous year
```

Understanding item comparison

Item comparison is used to take any item on any financial statement and compare it with the same item in the previous year, or in previous years. This is usually done for costs, sales and items of expense.

This is a simple measure, showing how far items have changed. If legal fees were £17.3 million in one year and £24.9 million in the next year, the ratio gives us 1.44. By subtracting 1 and multiplying by 100, we convert this to a percentage increase of 44%.

How to use item comparison as an investor

Item comparison may be employed for an item where the increase (or sometimes, decrease) appears particularly large.

In general, most items in financial statements should move by similar ratios. If there has been a 10% increase in sales, it is reasonable to expect a 10% increase in the costs of producing those sales and similar increases for expenses. Some expenses will tend not to vary so much. Examples include insurance and the audit fee.

A significant change may justify investigation. A large increase in an expense could be an early warning of an expensive legal action, problems with a new product, inefficient management or similar.

Where an item comparison does indicate a possible problem, look at the narrative reports to see if there is any reference to the matter. If the company incurred high expenses in marketing a faulty product, that should be mentioned in the directors' report or chairman's report. Such an eventuality does not make the company a poor investment, as most companies can accommodate a few failures as part of the price of success. The investor needs to be satisfied that the expense is either justified or adequately explained.

Variations on item comparison

Intercompany comparisons

Intercompany comparisons can be made on a similar basis to item comparisons within one company, such as by comparing margins between similar companies. The main consideration here is that no two companies are ever identical in their management policies or circumstances. One company may have a policy of low margins and high volume; another may spend heavily on research to ensure a steady flow of future products. Such differences must always be allowed for in intercompany comparisons.

Divisional comparisons

Divisional comparisons look at how different parts of the group compare. Most public companies trade as a group of companies. This means that there is a parent company and many other limited companies that are subsidiaries of this parent company. Sometimes the subsidiaries themselves have sub-subsidiaries.

It is worth remembering that every separately constituted limited company must file accounts at Companies House. These accounts are publicly available, usually for a small fee. They give much greater detail than the consolidated accounts that are sent to shareholders or made otherwise readily available. Item comparisons and other ratios applied to these accounts can often indicate areas where there may be problems, or other factors that an investor should consider. There is a practical problem in that such accounts are often filed after the group accounts.

8

Policy Ratios

8.1

Creditor Period

Definition

```
Creditor period = (trade creditors ÷ cost of sales) x 365
```

Creditor period is sometimes also known as **creditor days**.

Trade creditors is money the company owes to its trade suppliers on the last day of the accounting period.

It should be noted that this figure should only include creditors who supply goods which the company sells or which the company uses to make goods it sells. So other creditors should be excluded. This includes creditors who supply fixed assets, stationery, insurance and all other forms of overheads. In practice, the balance sheet may not distinguish between trade creditors and non-trade creditors. Where the non-trade creditors are small, and where they are likely to be similar from year-to-year, their inclusion is unlikely to affect what the ratio indicates.

Cost of sales is the figure subtracted from sales to give gross profit, as shown in the profit and loss account.

Understanding the creditor period

The creditor period is the average number of days it takes the company to pay its bills.

Unlike most other accounting ratios, creditor period measures policy rather than performance. Creditor period does not so much measure how well a company has done but what it has decided to do.

A company must state its policy for paying creditors in the directors' report. A typical comment is "we pay our creditors within the agreed terms".

The creditor period can both test the credibility of such statements and determine what that policy is. A large company is in a position to bully a smaller supplier into accepting long payment terms. Accusations of this kind have been made against supermarkets. A lengthening credit period could indicate such bullying.

Most agreed credit periods are typically 30 to 60 days, so anything longer than this indicates that the company could be taking advantage of its creditors. A credit period shorter than this could indicate that the company has difficulties obtaining supplies on normal trade terms.

How to use creditor period as an investor

At first sight, the creditor period may seem completely irrelevant to the investor. If the company can get away with taking a bit longer to pay its bills, why should the investor worry? Even if the company is borrowing money at a high rate of 8%, taking one extra month to pay a bill results in a saving to the company of less than 0.7%. If the net profit margin is only 15%, taking an extra month could add another 2% (to make the margin 17%).

The creditor period is useful for comparison with companies in the same sector and of a similar size, and for determining trends.

A lengthening creditor period is often caused by a company getting into financial difficulties. So a higher creditor period than a competitor, or a trend of lengthening periods, can be an early warning sign of financial problems.

If the accounts reveal healthy profits and plenty of ready cash, higher creditor periods or lengthening periods could indicate bullying by the company. Typically such policies only provide a benefit in the short term. Losing supplier goodwill can quickly lead to higher prices, as suppliers build in the cost of credit. It can also mean that the suppliers are less willing to be helpful to the company. How far this could affect the company depends on many circumstances, most of which are likely not to be known by the investor.

In many companies, the creditor period has little value, even though it can be calculated. Where a company derives most of its value internally (as in service companies), the creditor period is of especially little use.

8.2
Debtor Period

Definition

```
Debtor period = (trade debtors ÷ sales) x 365
```

Trade debtors is the amount owed to the company by its customers at the end of the year. Strictly speaking, this excludes debtors who are not customers. In practice, this figure is usually small, representing perhaps unpaid rent and deposits awaiting return. The balance sheet figure for debtors usually includes prepayments. Again, the amounts are likely to be small.

In practice, the balance sheet figure for **debtors** (or **accounts receivable** or **receivables**) is likely to be good enough for these purposes. Non-trade debtors are likely to be small enough that any amounts will largely be cancelled out in any comparison or trend detection.

Sales is the revenue from selling goods or services (as explained in Chapter 4).

Understanding the debtor period

The debtor period is the average time a customer takes to pay an invoice.

Mathematically, the debtor period is simply the corollary of the creditor period, explained above. However, to the investor it is more of an efficiency ratio than a policy ratio. The company decides when to pay its own bills, but cannot so readily determine when its customers pay theirs.

It can be a measure of efficiency, as effective credit control can reduce the debtor period by about 30 days.

How to use the debtor period as an investor

As with most accounting ratios, it is necessary to understand the business. A supermarket, restaurant or other business that deals directly with the public should have a very short debtor period. Construction companies will have a longer period. The debtor period is of little value for cash businesses.

The ratio may also be used to detect trends and for comparison with companies in the same sector.

A **deterioration** in debtor period is of particular concern. It could indicate that the company is failing in its credit control or that it is gaining new and less creditworthy customers.

Another even more worrying explanation is that the company itself is less creditworthy and is **anticipating profit.** Many companies from the scandal-ridden Enron to the established cider maker Bulmer have been found to have booked profits before they should have done. My Travel and Allied Carpets have both been required to restate accounts for this reason.

Booking profits early has the effect of increasing the sales figure, indicating a greater level of success. However this has a disproportionately large effect on debtors.

A deteriorating debtor period could also indicate a growing incidence of **bad debts.** These are debts that are never paid, usually because the customer becomes insolvent. It should be noted that bad debts do not affect either the sales or gross profit figure. This is because bad debts are treated as an expense or overhead.

8.3
Fixed Asset Spending Ratio

Definition

```
Fixed asset spending ratio = fixed asset spending ÷
                                  annual depreciation
```

Fixed asset spending is the amount the company has spent acquiring new fixed assets during the year. Fixed assets are items worth money and which are expected to last for more than one year. Examples include land, buildings, plant, machinery, furniture and vehicles.

In accounting, such a fixed asset is usually included in the balance sheet at the price paid for it. If a new lathe is acquired by an engineering company for £10,000, the amount paid for the lathe plus related costs, such as delivery and installation, is regarded as a fixed asset. Such costs are said to be **capitalised**. That means that they are not listed as an expense in the profit and loss account. The company does not say that it has spent this £10,000 in the year as it still has the lathe which will help the company to earn a profit.

The company then estimates the useful life of the fixed asset. Suppose it believes that the lathe will last ten years. It will then calculate **depreciation** on the cost. It may deduct £1000 in the first year. This is shown in the profit and loss account as an expense for that year and for each subsequent year. The value of the lathe will be included in the figure for fixed assets in the balance sheet, at £9000 in the first year, £8000 in the second year and so on.

The only exception to the policy of depreciating fixed assets is **land**. This is never depreciated, though the cost of buildings on them is depreciated. As buildings often *appreciate* in value, this depreciated value is then often increased again by a revaluation. However, such revaluation is generally not relevant for this ratio as it is not included in either spending or depreciation.

Understanding the fixed asset spending ratio

The fixed asset spending ratio indicates how far the company is maintaining its ability to continue trading and earning profits. On this basis, a ratio of 1 or above indicates a healthy state.

Depreciation means that the company has used up or worn out a certain amount of the value of its fixed assets. The spending figure indicates how much of this has been replaced.

How to use the fixed asset spending ratio as an investor

This ratio provides a simple measure that usually gives a reliable indicator of how a business is being managed for future years. A falling ratio could indicate a company that is getting into difficulties and is therefore cutting back on capital expenditure. Such a policy may provide a short-term palliative, but is likely to compromise the ability of the company to earn future profits.

The ratio is likely to give an accurate indicator where the fixed assets comprise large amounts of **machinery** (including vehicles). If a factory has 100 lathes, the ratio should give an accurate indication of how far the company is replacing lathes as they wear out.

For other types of fixed asset, the ratio is less accurate. **Computer equipment**, for example, is becoming much cheaper. A computer sold for £500 in 2010 has much greater capacity and power than one costing £5000 in 1995. So a ratio of 0.5 for computer equipment could still indicate full replacement of fixed assets.

For **property**, there are special considerations. Revaluation has no effect on the ratio in the year it is undertaken, but it does affect the ratio in future years.

Suppose a company has a freehold property worth £20 million. It decides that the land is worth £8 million and the building standing on the land is worth £12 million. Only the latter figure is depreciated. Typically a building is depreciated over 50 years, which means that £240,000 each year is added to the expenses as depreciation and £240,000 is subtracted from the value each year. After three years, the land is still valued at £8 million and the building is valued at £11.28 million (which is £12 million minus £720,000).

Property is often revalued every three years. Suppose after three years, the land is valued at £10 million and the building at £13 million. This means that the fixed asset has increased by £2 million for the land and by £1.72 million for the building. This revaluation does not affect the ratio as these figures are not included in either element used to calculate the ratio.

However, in the following year the depreciation is calculated as one-fiftieth of £13 million, which is £260,000. Note that the increase in the land value does not affect the depreciation of this ratio.

In itself this increased depreciation should not affect the ratio except to improve its reliability. If the building is now losing value at £260,000 each year, it is reasonable to expect the company to be spending a similar figure to maintain the adequacy of its premises.

What is relevant for the investor is that he or she understands what lies behind the figures used in this ratio.

9

Volatility

9.1
Volatility Ratio

Definition

```
Volatility = (((Period high - period low) ÷ 2) ÷ current
                                  share price) x 100
```

Period high means the highest price at which that share has been traded during the period. This is usually shown in the *Financial Times* as *high*.

Period low is the lowest price for which that share has been traded during the period. This is similarly indicated in lists of share prices.

Subtracting the low from the high and dividing by two gives the average amount (in pence) by which the share price has deviated from its average.

Suppose a share has a high of 120p and a low of 90p. The figure for (period high – period low) ÷ 2 is 15p, which is half the difference of 30p. This means that the share price was never more than 15p away from the average of its high and low price during the period. Note that this does not mean that the average share price for the period was 105p. The share price could have been near its high or low for most of the year and hit the opposite extreme near the year-end.

Current share price is the price currently being quoted for the share.

If, in our example, the current share price is 110p, the volatility is calculated as:

```
(((120 - 90) ÷ 2) ÷ 110) x 100 = 13.6%
```

Understanding volatility

Volatility measures the fluctuation in the share price. In other words, it measures how much the share fluctuates in value. The higher the volatility, the less stable is the share.

Share prices are affected by many different factors. At its simplest these can be distinguished between those that affect the stock market as a whole and those that affect that share in particular. The simplest way to distinguish these two sets of factors is to ascertain the volatility of the market as a whole and compare it with that for the share. Historically, any market move above 2% was considered volatile. In the more turbulent times since 2000, much larger swings have occurred almost routinely.

How to use volatility as an investor

The more volatile a share is, the greater is the risk in owning it. Whether this makes it a good investment depends on the investor's investment strategy, such as to the extent that an investor diversifies the holding. This is considered in Chapter 5.

What an investor really wishes to know is the **future** value of the shares, or the probability of the shares reaching a particular value or range of values. Past share prices are not always a reliable indicator of future prices, or even of the direction of future prices.

The volatility ratio described here is sometimes called **historic volatility** to distinguish it from the future volatility, which is of more concern to the investor. Sophisticated mathematical models have been developed, particularly for share options and other financial derivatives. This is a specialist area of mathematics for specialist investors, such as hedge funds.

The simpler approach is for the investor to realise that a share price of a listed company is basically dependent on two sets of factors:

• how the stock market as a whole performs, and

• how the company itself performs.

The former is little more than guesswork, as is evidenced by the fact that none of the turbulent rises and falls since 1999 have been predicted with any accuracy by any expert, despite what they may say with hindsight. If you believe the stock market is about to perform very badly, the only decision for an investor is whether to stay in the market at all, not whether to swap shareholdings. An investor may decide to invest in cash until the turbulence is over. An alternative policy is simply to hold tight and wait.

The latter – how the company itself performs – requires analysis beyond number-crunching. The investor must look at the state of the economy, which involves consideration of economics and politics.

An investor should always remember that volatility is a short-term measure. There is often an adverse correlation that a short-term stable investment represents a long-term risk. Sadly the converse is not also true – an investment that is volatile in the short-term is not necessarily stable in the long term. When looking outside shares, investments can easily be manipulated to appear stable and conceal their true volatility.

9.2
Standard Deviation

Standard deviation was developed as a mathematical tool in 1894.

Definition

$$\sigma = \sqrt{\frac{\sum(x - \bar{X})^2}{n}}$$

where

σ = standard deviation

x = the average (arithmetic mean) share price;

$\bar{x}$ = the share price at the end of a particular day;

n = the number of share prices

(The formula is sometimes stated with *n* - 1, instead of *n*.)

In practice, the calculation involves five steps:

1. Calculate the amount by which each day's closing price differs from the average.
2. Square each answer.
3. Add up the squares.
4. Divide by the number of answers.
5. Take the square root.

Let's consider a simple example.

Example: standard deviation

Share A has these closing prices over four days:

96, 103, 101, 100.

Share B has these closing prices:

80, 92, 130, 98.

Each of these share prices have an average of 100, but it is immediately obvious that Share B has greater variation and is therefore more volatile.

The differences between the daily closing prices and the four-day average share price for Share A are -4, +3, +1, 0. (The + and – do not matter as they disappear when the number is squared.) The squares are 16, 9, 1 and 0. These total 26. Divided by 4, this equals 6.5, of which the square root is **2.45**.

For Share B, the differences between the daily closing prices and the four-day average share price are -20, -8, +30, -2. The squares are 400, 64, 900 and 4. These total 1368. Dividing by 4, this equals 342, of which the square root is **18.49**.

So, the standard deviation for Share A is 2.45 and the standard deviation for share B is 18.49.

The standard deviation may be used statistically to indicate the likelihood of a particular price differing from the average on a given day. Using the standard bell-shaped probability curve, there is a:

- 68.2% probability that the share price will differ from the average by no more than the standard deviation.

- 95.4% probability it will differ by no more than twice the standard deviation.

- 99.8% probability it will differ by no more than three times the standard deviation.

For example, for our shares A and B, this means there is a 68.2% probability that the closing price of share A will differ from its average by no more than 2.45 on a given day and there is a 95.4% probability that share B will differ from its average by no more than 36.98 (2 x 18.49) on a given day.

Understanding standard deviation

Standard deviation measures the dispersion within a series of numbers. It tells you how far a series of numbers strays from the average. A high number indicates a big dispersion which means that the share is more volatile than a lower number.

In practice, this calculation is tedious unless done by a computer. This can be done by using a scientific calculator or a spreadsheet. (The indicator for Microsoft Excel is STDEV.)

The standard deviation is very accurate and capable of being used for further mathematical analysis (such as in probability, as explained above). It is also versatile in that an accurate figure can be calculated for a large population by using randomly selected numbers. There is even a formula to determine how many random numbers to select.

The volatility ratio differs from the standard deviation in two important respects:

1. It only considers the highest and lowest share prices.

2. It relates the variation to the *current* share price, rather than the average.

The second point means that a falling share price will show a greater volatility than a rising share price, whereas the standard deviation is the same.

In our examples, the volatility ratio of shares A and B is 7% and 31.25% respectively.

How to use standard deviation as an investor

The extent to which an investor even considers standard deviation is probably dependent on the investor's mathematical education. For those who do understand the mathematics, there is a danger that statistics do not tell you something new, but simply tell you what you already know, but more precisely.

In reality, an investor is unlikely to care whether a share is 91.2% likely to increase by 34.6%, but is content with knowing that the share will probably increase in value by about one-third in a defined period. In short, there is no point in calculating standard deviation unless you are going on to further mathematical analysis.

Standard deviation is widely used in financial models such as **mean variance optimisation**. Chapter 5 explains the concept of risk and reward; standard deviation provides a mathematical basis for implementing such a policy.

This optimisation requires the investor to determine a **risk and reward policy**. For example, if share C indicates a 10% return and 11% standard deviation, whereas share D indicates a 12% return but a 19% standard deviation, the investor must decide whether the probability of another 2% return with share D is worth the additional 8% standard deviation.

A very rough rule of thumb could be to subtract twice the standard deviation from the return and go for the higher number, which may be negative. In our example, this would be:

Share C: 10 – 22 = -12

Share D: 12 – 38 = -26

So share C accords with the investor's strategy of placing great significance on volatility. (Such a calculation could also be performed using the volatility ratio.)

In practice, an investor is unlikely to use such a simplistic formula if he or she has gone to the effort to calculate the standard deviation in

the first place. However, it may be useful if the standard deviation has already been calculated.

The above rule of thumb illustrates how a volatility ratio can be mathematically equated with return to reflect an investment policy. Fund managers can programme these into computers to trigger automatic buying and selling instructions.

Variation on standard deviation

A variation on standard deviation is **mean absolute deviation**.

The formula is:

$$\text{Mean absolute deviation} = \frac{\sum(x - \overline{X})}{n}$$

This is the formula for standard deviation, but without the square and square root. It is simpler to calculate. If calculation is a problem, this measure will perform a similar function as standard deviation. However, it has the disadvantages of being less versatile in that it cannot be used as the basis for further calculation.

Appendix

The list below indicates those ratios which may be of particular benefit to an investor in particular circumstances or against particular criteria (figures in brackets indicate the part of the book where this ratio is discussed).

Ability to raise capital

Return on assets (2.7)
Gearing (5.1)
Overtrading and undertrading (7.3)

Capital usage

Return on capital employed (2.3)
Return on equity (2.4)
Gearing (5.1)

Cash flow

Debtor period (8.2)

Comparison with other companies

P/E ratio (1.2)
Stock turn (7.1)
Item comparison (7.4)

Comparison with other investments

Dividend yield (2.1)
Total return (2.2)
Internal rate of return (2.6)

Efficiency

Return on capital employed (2.3)
Stock turn (7.1)

Future performance

Forward P/E (1.2)
Future yield (2.1)
Acid test (6.1)
Fixed asset spending ratio (8.3)

Growing companies

EV/EBITDA (1.3)
Gearing (5.1)

Health of company

Dividend yield (2.1)

Investment potential

P/E ratio (1.2)
Dividend yield (2.1)
Total return (2.2)
Return on equity (2.4)

Long-term investments

Dividend cover (3.1)

Loss-making companies

EV/EBITDA (1.3)
Price-to-Sales (1.4)

Management

Net profit (4.1)
Overheads to turnover (4.2)
Stock turn (7.1)
Overtrading and undertrading (7.3)
Item comparison (7.4)
Debtor period (8.2)
Fixed asset spending ratio (8.3)

Market expectation

P/E ratio (1.2)
Premium to asset value (2.5)

Past performance

Earnings per share (1.1)
Return on assets (2.7)
Overheads to turnover (4.2)

Performance

Dividend payout ratio (2.8)
Net profit (4.1)
Price-to-Book value (7.2)
Overtrading and undertrading (7.3)

Policy

Dividend payout ratio (2.8)
Gross profit (4.1)

Interest cover (5.2)
Creditor period (8.1)

Profitability

Earnings per share (1.1)
P/E ratio (1.2)
EV/EBITDA (1.3)
Price-to-Sales (1.4)
Return on capital employed (2.3)
Return on equity (2.4)
Net profit (4.1)
Interest cover (5.2)

Profit sustainability

Price-to-Sales (1.4)
Return on assets (2.7)
Dividend payout ratio (2.8)
Dividend cover (3.1)
Interest cover (5.2)
Fixed charges cover (6.5)
Creditor period (8.1)

Return on investment

Earnings per share (1.1)
Total return (2.2)
Return on capital employed (2.3)
Internal rate of return (2.6)

Share valuation

Price-to-Sales (1.4)
Price-to-Book value (7.2)

Solvency

Interest cover (5.2)
Acid test (6.1)
Current ratio (6.2)
Cash burn (6.3)
Defensive interval (6.4)
Fixed charges cover (6.5)

Start-up companies

EV/EBITDA (1.3)
Cash burn (6.3)
Defensive interval (6.4)

Valuation

Premium to asset value (2.5)
Price-to-Book value (7.2)

Volatility

Volatility ratio (9.1)
Standard deviation (9.2)

Index

A

accounting practice 6, 86
accounting standards
    changes in ix
    FRS 14 5, 8
    FRS 18 96-97
    FRS 4 82
    IAS 33 5, 6
    SSAP 3 6
Accounting Standards Board (ASB)
    6, 8
accounts
    consolidated vii
    copies, obtaining viii
    receivable 131
acid test 95-98
    cash flow, and 97-98
    definition 95
    niche companies, and 98
    ratio 95
    understanding 96-97
    using as an investor 97-98
    yardstick 97
activity, knowledge of x
amortisation 22

Annual Reports Service viii
annual sales 25
anticipating profit 132
appreciation 134
ASB, *see* 'Accounting Standards
    Board'

B

bad debts 132
bank view of companies 60
bonus issue 5
break-even point 76
burn rate 101
Business Link 106

C

capital
    at start of year 101
    available 117-118
    gains tax (CGT) 38
    required 117
    structure 84
    usage 149
capital growth
    definition of 37
    dividend cover, and 67

capitalisation 133
capitalised costs 133
cash
    expenditure, year's 101
    flow 97, 149
    gearing, and 82
    negative 97
    positive 97
cash burn 10, 22, 101-103
    business, types of 101
    definition 101
    EV/EBITDA, and 103
    understanding 101-103
    using as an investor 103
cd, *see* 'cum div' 31
CGT, *see* 'capital'
Companies House viii
company
    growth 150
    health 150
    loss-making 151
    start-up 153
comparability ix
comparison viii, 121
    companies, other 149
    investments, other 150
computer equipment 134
consolidated accounts vii
convertible preference shares 10, 87
cost of sales 111, 127
creditor period 127-129
    definition 127
    understanding 128
    using as an investor 128-129
creditors 96

creditors due within one year 96
cum div 31
cumulative preference shares 87
current
    assets 95, 99
    liabilities 96, 99
    share price 139
current ratio 99-100
    definition 99
    understanding 99-100
    using as an investor 100

D

daily operating expenses 105
debt funding 82
debtor period 131-132
    anticipating profits 132
    bad debts 132
    credit control 132
    definition 131
    deterioration in 132
    understanding 131-132
    using as an investor 132
debtors 131
defensive interval 105-106
    cash flow 106
    definition 105
    understanding 105-106
    using as an investor 106
depreciation 22, 133
diluted EPS
    calculation of 5-6
    considered 10
    defined 5
discount to asset value 51
dividend

cum div 31
  definition 31, 32
  ex div 31
  interim 31
  paid to 31
  per share 61
  policy 35
  record 34
  share price, effect on 31
dividend cover 65-67
  capital growth, and 67
  definition 65
  dividend yield, and 66
  eps, and 66
  income, and 66
  policy 89
  sustainability 65
  understanding 65-66
  using as an investor 66-67
dividend payout ratio 61-62
  definition 61
  retained earning ratio 62
  understanding 61-62
  using as an investor 62
  variations on 62
dividend yield 9, 31-35
  company health, and 34
  comparison, as a 34
  definition 31
  dividend cover, and 66
  future yield 35
  measure, as a 33
  on purchase price 37
  policy 35
  record, previous 34

  tax implications 32-33
  understanding 32-33
  usage not possible 33
  using as an investor 34-35
  variations on 35
  yield 31, 33
divisional comparisons 122-123

E

E/P, see 'price-to-earnings'
earnings multiple, see 'price-to-earnings'
earnings per share 3-11
  definition 3
  diluted 5-6, 10-11
  directional 8
  gearing, and 84-85
  negative, significance of 10
  smoothing of 11
  understanding 7-8
  undiluted 10-11
  using as an investor 8-11
  variation over time 11
EBITDA, see 'EV/EBITDA'
efficiency ratios 111, 150, see:
  item comparison
  overtrading
  price to book value (PBV)
  stock turn
  undertrading
efficiency: profit 74
enterprise value, definition 21
  see also 'EV/EBITDA'
EPS, see 'earnings per share'
equity 47
equity funding 82

established company: gearing 86
EV/EBITDA 21-23
    amortisation 22
    cash burn, and 103
    definition 21, 22
    depreciation 22
    positive 22-23
    profits, and 22-23
    understanding 22-23
    using as an investor 23
ex div 31
expense ratio 78

F

fixed asset spending 133-135
    appreciation 134
    computer equipment 134
    definition 133
    depreciation 134
    machinery 134
    property 135
    understanding 134
    using as an investor 134-135
fixed charges 107
fixed charges cover 107-108
    definition 107
    understanding 108
    using as an investor 108
forced realisation 97
Forward P/E (P/Ef) 17-18
FRS 14, *see* 'accounting standards'
FRS 18, *see* 'accounting standards'
FRS 4, *see* 'accounting standards'
future
    performance 150
    yield 35

G

gearing ratio 81-88
    comparison, as a 86
    debt equity, nature of 87-88
    debt funding 82
    definition 81
    eps, and 84-85
    established companies, and 86
    example of 83-85
    high gearing
        interpreting 86-87
        positive, as a 88
    new companies, and 86
    preference shares 87
    understanding 82-85
    using as an investor 86-88
    volatility, and 87
going concern, concept of 96
goodwill 26, 51
gross
    loss 73
    profit 71
    profit margin 73
gross margin 71-76
    definition 71
    gross loss 73
    gross profit margin 73
    periods 73
    understanding 72-73
    using as an investor 73-75
    trends in 75
    variations on 76
    what to look for 73
grossed up, definition of 32
growing companies 150

H

historic volatility 140

I

IAS 33 6
individual savings account, *see* 'ISA'
intercompany comparisons 122
interest
    covenants 90
    definition 3
    paid 89
    rates, variable 87
    sensitivity 90
interest cover 89-91
    definition 89
    interest
        covenants 90
        sensitivity 90
    gearing, and 90
    poor trading 90
    price wars 91
    understanding 89-90
    using as an investor 90-91
internal rate of return (IRR) 55-58
    definition 55
    iteration 55
    risk 57-58
    rule of 72 57
    understanding 56-57
    using as an investor 57-58
investment
    good? x-xi, 8, 15
    long-term 150
    potential 150
    strategy xi

    trusts 38
investment ratios, *see*:
    dividend payout ratio
    dividend yield
    internal rate of return (IRR)
    premium to asset value (PAV)
    return on assets (ROA)
    return on capital employed
        (ROCE)
    return on equity (ROE)
    total return
IRR, *see* 'internal rate of return'
ISAs, tax and 33
item comparison 121-123
    definition 121
    understanding 121
    using as an investor 121-122
    variations on 122-123
iteration 55

J

junk bond 88

L

land 134
liquid assets 105
liquidity 100
    ratio 95

M

machinery 134
management 151
market
    capitalisation 21, 25, 26, 115
    expectation 151
    perception xi

Market P/E, *see* 'price-to-earnings'
  mean
    absolute deviation 147
    variance optimisation 146
minority interests, definition of 3-4
multiple, *see* 'price-to-earnings'

N

NAV, *see* 'net'
NCE, *see* 'net - capital employed'
negative EPS 10
net
  asset value (NAV) 51, 52
  assets 26, 47, 59, 115
  capital employed (NCE) 41, 44
  operating profit less adjusted
    taxes 42
  profit 3, 59, 71
  profit attributable to
    shareholders 47
  profit before fixed charges 107
  profit margin 74
    as a measure of efficiency 75-
    76
  tangible asset value (NTA) 51,
    115
net margin 71-76
  definition 71
  net profit margin 74
    as a measure of efficiency 75-
    76
  periods 73
  trends in 75
  understanding 72-73
  using as an investor 73-75
  variations on 76

  what to look for 73
NOPLAT 42
NTA, *see* 'net'
number of shares
  complications with 4-5
  definition of 4
  in issue 52

O

operating margin 76
organic growth 86
overall return on current value 39-
  40
overcapitalisation 117
overheads 77
overheads to turnover 77-78
  definition 77
  understanding 77-78
  variations on 78
overtrading, 117-119
  creditor days, and 118
  current ratio, and 118
  debtor days, and 118
  definition 117
  turnover ratios, and 118
  understanding 117-118
  using as an investor 119

P

P/E 10, *see* 'price-to-earnings'
P/E from continued operations, *see*
  'price-to-earnings'
P/E ratio, *see* 'price-to-earnings'
P/Ef, *see* 'Forward P/E'
PAV, *see* 'premium to asset value'
PBV, *see* 'price-to-book value'

Index

PEG, *see* 'price-to-earnings growth
    ratio'
PER, *see* 'price-to-earnings'
performance 151
    past 151
period 73
    high 139
    low 139
plant 134
policy 151-152
policy ratios 125, *see*:
    creditor period
    debtor period
    fixed asset spending ratio
positive PAV 53
premium to asset value 51-53
    definition 51
    discount to asset value 51
    understanding 52
    using as an investor 52-53
Present Value of Growth
    Opportunities (PVGO), *see*
    'price-to-earnings'
pre-tax
    margin 76
    profit 89
price-to-book value (PBV) 115-116
    definition 115
    understanding 116
    using as an investor 116
price to sales ratio 22, 25
price war 91
price-to-earnings (P/E)
    comparison, as a
        investments, other 17

    shares 16
    definition 13
    E/P 18
    earnings multiple 13
    Forward P/E 17-18
    interpreting
        by sector 15
        values 15-16
    Market P/E 18
    multiple 13
    negative 14
    P/E 10 18
    P/E TTM 13
    P/E from continued operations
        18
    PEG 17
    PER 13
    PVGO 19
    ratio 7, 10, 13-19
    understanding 13-14
    unlisted companies 14
    using as an investor 15-16
    variations on 17-19
price-to-earnings growth (PEG) 17
price-to sales (PSR) 25-27
    definition 25
    revenue multiple 25
    understanding 26
    using as an investor 27
profit
    anticipation 132
    before interest and tax 41
    margins 71-76
        trends in 75
    pre-tax 89

161

retained, see 'retained profit'

profitability 152

    sustainability 152

profitability ratios, see:

    earnings per share (EPS)

    enterprise value/earnings before
        interest, taxes,
        depreciation and
        amortisation
        (EV/EBITDA)

    price-to-earnings (P/E)

    price-to sales (PSR)

property 135

PSR, see 'price-to sales'

PVGO, see 'price-to-earnings'

Q

quick

    assets 96

    ratio 95

R

raising capital 149

ratios

    accounting vii

    calculating vii-viii

    comparing viii-ix

    defined vii

    how to use them x-xi

    interpretation of xi

    junkies x

    reliance on ix

    trends ix

    understanding viii-ix

receivables 131

reserves 7

Retail Prices Index 87

retained

    earnings ratio 62

    profit (eps) 7-8, 9

    profit

        defined 7

        indictor, as 9

    assets 59

    average capital employed 44

    average equity 49

    equity 47

    investment (eps) 9

return on assets (ROA) 59-60

    banks, and 60

    definition 59

    profits 60

    trend plotting, for 60

    turnover per employee 60

    understanding 59

    using as an investor 59-60

    variations on 60

return on average capital employed
        (ROACE) 44

return on average equity (ROAE)
        49

return on capital employed (ROCE)
        41-45

    assets, and 42

    definition 41

    excluding cash 45

    goodwill, and 42

    NOPLAT 42

    trading activities, on 44

    understanding 42

    using as an investor 43

variations on 44-45

return on equity (ROE) 47-49
  business type, and 48
  definition 47
  understanding 48
  using as an investor 48-49
  variations on 49

return on investment 152

revenue 25, 72

revenue multiple, *see* 'price-to sales'

rising profits: gearing 88

risk and reward 88
  policy 146

risk in start-ups 57

ROA, *see* 'return on assets'

ROACE 44

ROAE 49

ROCE, *see* 'return on capital
        employed'

ROE, *see* 'return on equity'

ROI, *see* 'return on investment'

root, calculating 40

rule of 72 57

S

sales 25, 72, 111, 131

sales revenue 72

shareholders'
  equity 47, 115
  funds 47, 51, 82

share price, definition of 13, 25, 32,
        51
  current 139

share valuation 152

smaller companies P/E 16

smoothing out EPS 11

solvency 153

solvency ratios 96, 100, *see*:
  acid test
  cash burn
  current ratio
  defensive interval
  fixed charges cover

SSAP 3 6

standard deviation 143-147
  definition 143
  example 144-145
  mean absolute deviation 147
  mean variance optimisation 146
  risk and reward policy
  understanding 145
  using as an investor 146-147
  variations on 147

start-up risk 57

stock 95, 111

stock days 111, 113

stock turn 111-113
  definition 111
  stock days 111, 113
  trends 112
  understanding 111-112
  using as an investor 112
  variations on 113

subsidiaries vii

T

tax, definition of 3

total
  borrowings 81-82
  return on current value 39

total return 37-40
  comparison, as a 38

definition of 37

investment trusts, and 38

on current value 39

overall return on current value 39-40

understanding 38

using as an investor 38

variations on 39

trade

creditors 127

debtors 131

knowledge of x

trading stamp companies 97

trailing P/E 13

trends ix

turnover 25, 72, 77

per employee 60

U

undercapitalisation 117

undertrading, 117-119

definition 117

understanding 117-118

using as an investor 119

undiluted eps 10-11

unlisted companies (P/E) 14

V

valuation 153

variable interest rates 87

volatility 87, 137, 153

volatility ratio 139-141

definition 139

future share value 140

historic volatility 140

understanding 140

using as an investor 140-141

W

weighted averages 4

X

xd, *see* 'ex div'

Y

year's cash expenditure 101

yield, *see* 'dividend yield'